JOURNEYS

BRIGANTIA

JOHN DIXON
AND
PHILLIP DIXON

<u>**VOLUME NINE:**</u>

THE RIBBLE VALLEY

Circular Walks "Twixt Bowland &
Pendle Where Rivers Meet'

JOURNEYS THROUGH BRIGANTIA
VOLUME NINE:
CIRCULAR WALKS IN THE RIBBLE VALLEY
"'TWIXT BOWLAND & PENDLE WHERE RIVERS MEET"

By

John Dixon & Phillip Dixon

Copyright © John Dixon & Phillip Dixon 1993
ALL RIGHTS RESERVED

Published by Aussteiger Publications,
8 Back Skipton Road, Barnoldswick BB8 5NE.
Tel. (0282) 812741

Typeset by:
Hargreaves Steel Limited,
133 Henry Street, Church, Accrington, Lancashire BB5 4EP

Printed by:
Lamberts of Settle

First edition, April 1993

ISBN 1 872764 05 3

The sketch maps in this book are intended to indicate the route in a general way. Walkers should use Ordnance Survey Pathfinder maps to locate exact routes.

Whilst all the walks use established and definitive footpaths (unless otherwise stated in the text), walkers are requested to respect the privacy of residents and not to stray from the footpaths.
If you find that a footpath has been obstructed, please report the matter on your return to: The County Surveyor, M. F. Callery, P.O. Box 9, Guild House, Preston PR1 8RD.

PLEASE OBSERVE THE COUNTRY CODE.

Dedicated to the 'Saturday Historic Walkers'.
In all weathers and throughout the years they have given me
their good support and valued friendship.
Thank you all — John

AUSSTEIGER PUBLICATIONS

Contents

AUSSTEIGER HISTORICAL FIELD GUIDES

Historic Walks around the Pendle Way   1990

JOURNEYS THROUGH BRIGANTIA

VOLUME ONE: 1990
Craven, Airedale & Wharfedale

VOLUME TWO: 1990
Ribblesdale, Malham & Central Wharfedale

VOLUME THREE:
Lower Wharfedale, Washburndale & Ilkley Moor

VOLUME FOUR: 1991
'Beyond the Hill of Winds': Upper Ribblesdale,
The Three Peaks & Upper Wharfedale

VOLUME FIVE:
Nidderdale, Knaresborough & Wensleydale

VOLUME SIX:
Swaledale, Teesdale & the Vale of Eden

VOLUME SEVEN:
The Lune Valley & The Howgill Fells

VOLUME EIGHT: 1992
The Forest of Bowland

VOLUME NINE: 1993
The Ribble Valley

VOLUME TEN:
Pendle & The Brönte South Pennines

VOLUME ELEVEN:
The East Lancashire Pennines

INTRODUCTION

Second only to Thwaites Bitter the River Ribble is Lancashire's premier flowing water. The valley it has cut offers a great variety of landscape from wild moorland tops to the rolling meadowland around the valley floor, a recognised Area of Outstanding Natural Beauty.

The area is bordered to the north-east by the Forest of Bowland, a wild upland area of heathery moors quartered by deep, steep-sided valleys. To the south-east Pendle rises leonine, her hind quarters resting in Whalley, her tail stretching over Billinge and her forepaws gripping Barnoldswick. Between these great formations snakes the River Ribble, on whose banks are to be found some of the great houses and mansions of yeoman Lancashire families.

The walking to be had is a rambler's delight. Footpaths along riverbanks, tracks over the moors, and peaceful country lanes passing villages that go back to pre-Conquest times. The landscape that your footfalls are guided through during the course of these rambles has been the home of man from the earliest times, back beyond recorded history. Only the burial sites and a few chance finds of artefacts testify to the presence and way of life of early man. This becomes most distinct in the area by the Ribble near Hacking Boat. Here two burials from that period known as the Middle Bronze Age were erected on the fertile valley floor near the confluences of the Ribble's major tributaries, the Hodder and the Calder.

The period between 1500-1000 BC was a renaissance in the development of early British peoples, a time of regular settlement patterns, new agricultural innovations, long distance trading, increased purchasing power and a formalisation of religious codes of practice. Man had now come down from his early upland Pennine settlements to clear the rich valley floors and lay the foundation for a way of life that was to dominate the next three thousand years. The modern villages of Whalley, Ribchester, Mellor Brook and Pendleton found their birth in these times.

By the arrival of Roman dominance, this now Iron Age Celtic society was organised on a pattern still reflected by pre-1974 parish boundaries — discreet multiple estates of two component parts: upland summer pasture and good arable land. Hence we have Clayton-le-Dale (arable) with Clayton-le-Moors (upland). Of the Roman occupation we have in the area more tangible evidence of their presence in the cavalry fort at Ribchester, sited on the crossroads of two of their major military ways.

The Medieval and early industrial periods have also left their mark on the valley. Ancient fortifications are to be found in farmyards, and old water mills are hidden in wooded dells. Each walk is a true exploration of former times, bringing alive the struggle and toil that has bred today's Lancashire folk. Good walking to you all.

— John Dixon, Barnoldswick, 1993

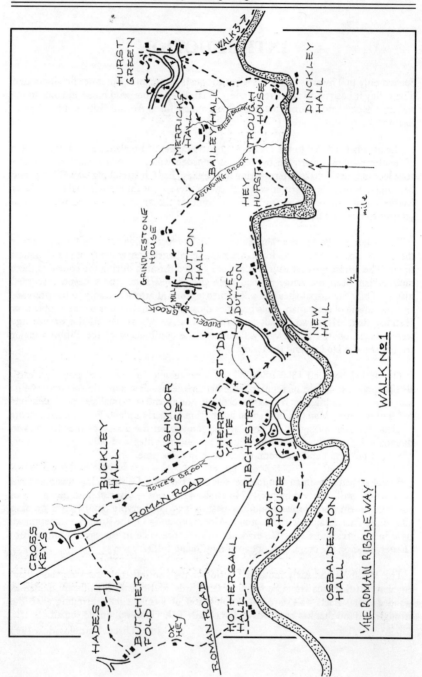

November '93

2 separate
walks

THE ROMAN RIBBLE WAY

Ribchester, Hothersall, Buckley, Stydd,
Hurst Green and Dutton

11 miles, 5 hours,
or two shorter walks of 5½ miles each

MAP: *O.S. sheet SD 63/73 PATHFINDER*

LUNCH: *White Bull, Ribchester, or*
               Bailey Arms, Hurst Green

START: *Ribchester Car Park or Hurst Green*

This "figure of 8" walk is one I use often to introduce folk to the splendid countryside and historic sites to be seen around Ribchester, not forgetting the Roman Fort site and the delightful village itself, being the focal points for most visitors. A visit to the Roman Museum and the Roman Bath House site will prove rewarding and complement this splendid ramble.

Ribchester

The village of Ribchester takes its name from the River Ribble and the Roman fort of Bremetennacum — "the walled town by the Ribble". Because of this fact, Ribchester has always been seen to have a purely Roman foundation, but excavations in 1977 have shown settlement going back to the Middle Bronze Age.

The site of the excavation was at the far end of the car park near the old people's home, and found here were five cremation burials in urns along with other Bronze Age material. The urns were seen to be deposited within a circular feature of some considerable size with a curving ditch surrounding the whole. As only a small section of the 'ring' was exposed, many other burials await discovery.

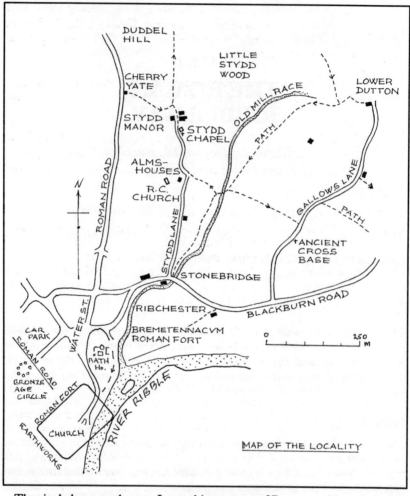

MAP OF THE LOCALITY

The site belongs to the east Lancashire pattern of Bronze and later Iron Age settlement, a network upon which the Roman army seems to have superimposed its roads and stations.

If we follow the route of the Roman road up from Manchester, we pass through numerous Bronze Age settlment sites in Bolton and Turton, then on to Darwen and Blackburn — both major Bronze and Iron Age territorial centres — then on to Mellor, the location of many early sites and finds.

Above Ribchester, following the road up towards the Hodder watershed, many settlement sites are encountered — Longridge Cairn Circle, the Bashall hut circles, Fairy Holes Caves, Easington Causewayed Camp and the Slaidburn burial mound being but a few.

The western and eastern roads from the fort also show many signs that they followed existing tracks established and used for many centuries before their arrival.

So, what do we really have at Ribchester? We have a major Bronze Age settlement site that probably saw continuity of settlement on through the Iron Age up to the arrival of the Romans who recognised the importance of the site and established a fort here.

This fort was first built in the latter part of the 1st century, with much rebuilding and alterations over the years. The fort was essentially an auxiliary cavalry garrison and two units are known to have been stationed there. The first of these was a wing of Asturian cavalry from Northern Spain. The famous Ribchester parade helmet has been ascribed to this garrison, although it could easily have come from a later period, perhaps kept by someone as an heirloom or some ceremonial object.

The second unit, the Sarmations from Hungary, arrived towards the end of the 2nd century. This unit was to stay on in the area, establishing a veteran settlement at Whalley from where they were later to administer the region.

This administration was based upon native Celtic lines of territorial land organisation, a process that remained intact in most of its structure until the 12th century. The Sarmations were well suited to settle in the area — being horse breeders by nature they would have found many common ties with the local Brigantian tribes, themselves being famed horsemen.

Throughout the Anglo-Celtic period, Ribchester is represented by the discovery of numerous artefacts, a silver gilt bracelet and an iron shield-boss, both of a 7th century date being good examples.

The Hiberno-Norse influence can be seen in the ornate decoration upon a beautiful bronze shield-boss and on the two fragments of stone cross-heads within the church.

During these pre-Conquest periods, Ribchester lost its former administrative status to Whalley and reverted to become a small collection of farmsteads with a manor house and possibly a church. The site of the post-Conquest manor house is in a field to the west of the now Manor Road. This was the home of the Moton family in the early 13th century, and the Lynalx in the late 14th.

Little of the Roman settlement remains to be seen at Ribchester today. The river and churchyard have taken most of the Roman fort from view, but a good museum displays many of the finds from the area along with the excavated remains of part of the Roman granaries. The latter, one must sadly report, is in a poor state, general neglect and elemental deterioration having taken their toll.

Another Roman feature to be viewed is the excavated Bath House, located at the rear of the White Bull. Recently erected explanation boards help one to pick out the outline of the bath house amid the crumbling piles of stones (the excavation was a costly disaster and much damage was done to floor tiles, walling etc.).

It consisted of a furnace room with three flues, the two southerly ones leading to the Caldarium (hot room) and the Tepidarium (warm room) respectively. The third leads to the Sudatorium (sweating room), this being round in shape. A fourth room on the south east of the building was the Frigidarium (cold room) with an apodyterium (changing room) adjacent to it. A stone-lined well stands on the south west corner of the site.

The building was erected in the 2nd century, with rebuilding work in later years. The whole structure was in use well into the late 4th century. On display inside the White Bull Hotel is a conjectural reconstruction in model form of what the bath house may have looked like in its heyday, along with a good example of a Samian ware bowl that was found hereabouts: Samian ware was first identified on the Greek island of Samos, hence its name.

It is a fine hard red ware, burnished, with moulded designs, produced and exported throughout the Empire from the potteries of Gaul. This 'terra sigillata' was mass produced tableware, developed in slightly simplified versions of originally Italian prototypes. This type of pottery predominated until the Gaulish factories were forced to close during the revolts of around 250.

With this the method of firing was lost, never to be rediscovered even to this day. Samian ware never ceases to amaze me — it looks as though it was made yesterday rather than nearly two thousand years ago. Truly we have lost a remarkable ceramic technique.

Little is known of the history of Ribchester during the seven hundred years after the departure of Roman authority in the early 5th century. What small 'tell-tale' signs remain must be sought within the local parish church of St. Wilfrid.

ST WILFRID'S CHURCH

Parish Church of St. Wilfrid

For the most part this is essentially a 13th century church. The chancel with its fine group of three stepped lancets — reminding one of the fate of three on a Friday afternoon at the Place of the Skull, Golgotha — is the best example. Remains of the original 12th century church can be found outside in the lower portion of the chancel wall. These represent the workmanship of the Norman transitional period, the stone displaying billet frieze being worthy of note.

In the north wall of the nave is a built-up doorway with a semi-circular arch that looks as though it could be Norman, but this is not so. Upon inspection I found it to be a re-used or badly repaired Early English piece.

Inside the church the first object of interest is the font. This is an octagonal piece with no decoration, only buttresses, possibly of the 14th century. Moving on into the north chapel, we can observe a good example of mediaeval wall painting depicting St. Christopher with the Holy Child. The window above the alter, a splendid example of curvilinear tracery of the Decorated period, contains fragments of late 14th century stained glass, once depicting Our Lord in Glory.

Moving from the Dutton Choir, we arrive at one of the most valued possessions of the church — the Jacobean pulpit. This is ornately Elizabethan in style, but dated 1636. We now move into the chancel to spy in the north wall what is said to be a Hagioscope or Leper's Squint, now considered to be an aumbrey (wall safe).

Moving to the south wall we notice the sedilia, providing three seats for the Celebrant and his assistants. Next to this is the piscina which is unusual, having a double bowl with floreated sinkings. Before leaving the chancel find, propped against the south wall, a mediaeval knight's grave-slab of the 12th century.

In the porch, along with two stone heads, can be found a plain Perpendicular tomb-chest with primitively carved shields. The picturesque sundial in the churchyard belongs to the early 18th century and stands on the base of what was originally the churchyard cross.

On a window ledge in the Dutton Choir chapel can be found two fragments of Anglo-Norse cross heads of a 10th century date. Also found on the fort site was a bronze Hiberno-Norse shield boss displaying a high standard of workmanship.

These objects lead us to the question of whether there was a pre-conquest foundation at Ribchester. The church stands within the walls of the Roman Fort of Bremetennacum, which in turn stands upon a settlement dating back to the Middle Bronze Age, so we could expect some continuity of settlement at Ribchester.

I think archaeologists and historians alike should pay more attention to the non-Roman aspects of Ribchester — only then shall we start to fill in those missing gaps in our past history.

This walk follows the Roman road which leads from Ribchester to their small supply fort at Kirkham. The road is recalled in many of the field-names along its length — Stroot Wood at Hothersall and Strait Meadow in Alston being good examples.

Ribchester to Hothersall Hall (follow Ribble Way signs)

Follow the riverbank lane on to pass through farmyard and on passing Lower Barn Farm and the Boat House (notice Osbaldeston Hall on the far side of the Ribble), through the gates and over the hill to drop down to a lane at Hothersall Hall via stile. Walk on into farmyard.

Ribchester Boat House and Ferry

The Ribchester ferry, which ran between below Ribchester and Osbaldeston Hall, is first mentioned in 1355 when Adam Bibby of Ribchester granted William de Braddeley 'fferiman' the right to carry people across the Ribble. Today the old boat house is a farm tenement, a reminder of a bygone age.

Hothersall Hall

The manor of Hothersall was granted to one Robert, who took the local name, in 1212 by King John when he was Count of Mortain.

The hall was rebuilt in 1856 in a plain Gothic style, on the site of the old house. No part of the former house remains, with the exception of a carved stone built into the wall of one of the outbuildings on which are the arms of the Hothersalls together with the initials T.H. (Thomas Hothersall) and the date 1695.

For his part in the Jacobite Rising of 1715, Thomas Hothersall along with Thomas Shuttleworth of Alston Old Hall, were executed.

In the fork of a tree on the lane above the hall can be found an horrific and grotesque stone head. This was dug up by a farmer at Hothersall and placed in its present position.

Some say that the head is that of the petrified Hothersall Boggart. Legend hereabouts informs us that a demon from Hades had undertaken to oblige a local farmer with three wishes for the surrender of his soul.

The farmer's first two wishes were for wealth and great fortune but his third was a crafty move to avoid damnation. He wished the devil to spin a rope from the sands of the Ribble and in case of failure he must consent to be laid (buried) under a laurel tree there to turn into stone (for a demon cannot rot, only fuse into granite etc.).

Each time the demon spun a rope the farmer poured water over the rope and it disintegrated. Eventually he gave up his efforts and accepted his fate, whereby the man of Hothersall escaped the devil's clutches and saved his soul. Though his head is secured in the bows of the tree, who is to say where the rest of this evil form roams, so beware the eve of the Moon when wandering in these parts.

Hothersall Hall to Hades

Walk up the driveway to go through field gate on right opposite "head" in tree and up to pass through higher gate. Walk up the field to pass through far gateway in hedge and directly on to enter walkway between high deer fences. Walk on to Ox Hey and on to the left to Butcher Fold. Pass through the farmyard and enter field and on along the track to pass through gate. Cross the field to pass over fence-stile and on to pass over stile at wood. Follow path

on to cross stream and stile and round to the left to the front of Hades farm via gate.

Hades Stone Heads

Set into the gable of the porch at Hades Farm are two fine 'Celtic' heads. The owners have no knowledge of their origin, other than that they were once set into a low wall opposite the house. The lower head is more typically Celtic than the one above, having the wedge shaped nose and the oval eyes.

Hades is a strange name for a farmstead. I wonder if the heads are those of some poor damned farmers who fell foul of the Boggart of Hothersall?

Hades to Buckley Hall

Follow farm lane to road, right and on to turn left into Lord's Farm. Pass through farmyard by side of barn to pass through left hand field-gate and follow fence on to go through second gateway on left. Follow left hand fence to pass over stile and directly on to pass over next stile. Continue on to road via gate. Follow road to the right passing Greenmoor Lane to go down farm lane on left to Buckley Hall.

Buckley Hall

Now rebuilt in the Jacobean style to a very high standard, Buckley Hall as it now stands was well worth its resurrection from a mere original north wing. The majority of the original building was pulled down in 1895. Before that time it was a fine gabled stone house with mullioned windows. On the front of the building was inscribed:

NEW BUCKLEY IS MY NAME,
RIC SHERBVRNE BVILT THE SAME
ANNO 1662, AGED 62.

Richard was a son of Roger Shireburn of Buckley who died in 1605; Richard died without issue in 1674. This branch of the Shireburn family was descended from the Shireburns of Wolfen Hall above Chipping. In Richard's will, dated 1673, he desired to be buried 'in the quire at Chipping, belonging to my cousin, Robert Sherbourne, of Wolfhouse'.

The holding at Buckley was a composite one. Two messuages with land called the 'Hagges' were held of the king as of his Duchy of Lancaster by 200th part of a Knight's fee, half a rood of land was held by the 300th part of a fee, two acres called 'Spodspool' by the 200th part, and the rest by the 20th part of a fee.

A settlement is recited, made by Richard Shireburne, the father of Roger, in 1589-90, relating to the capital messuage called Buckley, and giving the names of the fields, farms and lanes, such as Turnley, Chester Gate and Kendal Heys.

Buckley Hall to Cherry Yate

Pass through yard and walk down the field to pass over stile in left corner. Walk down through the wood (the concrete pillar over on the left marks the site of a trial coal mine) to pass over footbridge and follow stream down to pass over next footbridge. Walk up to the left and on around Ashmoor House to follow the lane to Boyce's Farm. Pass over stile by gate opposite barn and walk past the dew pond down to go over footbridge. Walk on up to the roadway at Cherry Yate.

Cherry Yate

Cherry Yate was formerly Cherry Gate and, before that, Chester Gate, reflecting the old trackways of Lancashire.

The 1848 Ordnance Survey map marks the pedestal of an ancient cross at Cherry Gate. This, sadly, can no longer be found and all that remains of any ancient nature today are two inscribed stones. One bears the name "Cherry Yate", and another below this gives the date 1684 with the initials I.E.

Cherry Yate to Stydd Chapel

Walk up past Cherry Yate to pass over the stile on right. Walk down the field towards Stydd Manor Farm, through the farmyard and on to the Chapel.

Stydd Manor Farm

The farmhouse, known as Stydd Manor, is built on an artificial mound that was erected for some earlier structure. A stone above the front doorway bears the inscription REBECCA JOHN SHERBVRNE 1698 (or as some have recorded it ERECAT JOHN SHERBURNE 1698).

The raised mound upon which the house is built extends beyond the front garden towards Stydd Chapel and it was here that an archaeological excavation in 1912/13 revealed a remarkable find.

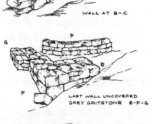

Whilst looking for the remains of the ancient Stydd Hospital of the Knights of St. John, the excavators laid bare the foundations of what is now held to be a Roman Mithreaum — a temple to the god Mithras.

Mithras was an eastern god who, according to legend, captured and killed the primaeval bull in a cave. From the slaying of this first creature created on earth sprang the benefits of mankind.

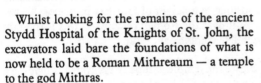

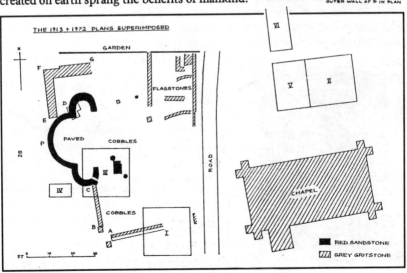

Thus mithraea were dark places purposefully resembling caves. Mithras was supported by his attendants, Cautes and Cautopotes. The cult was especially disliked by Christians who destroyed all temples in the 4th century.

This was undoubtedly what happened at Stydd. The foundation and dedication stone of the temple was found within the fort at Ribchester being used as a floor tile in a late Roman building.

The foundations of the temple were sited at a deep level and seen to be apsed to the western end. The existing walls were built of regular sandstone to a height of four feet in places. A later mediaeval building had been built over the Roman remains — this is thought to be connected with the Hospitalers complex at Stydd.

It is hoped that in the near future the temple will be re-excavated providing a much-needed Roman resource for visitors to Ribchester.

Stydd Chapel

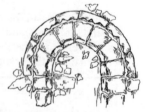

The earliest reference to the chapel and ancient hospital at Stydd is in the Quo Warranto proceedings of 1292 when it was proved that the Knights Hospitalers had acquired the estate around 1265 from Adam de Blackburn, chaplain-warden of the house of St. Saviour at Dutton under Longridge.

An undated charter (approximately 1150) informs us that Alan de Singleton confirmed land to the chapel and hospital. So Stydd had a very early foundation indeed. This is reflected by the Norman doorway and windows in the north wall.

The majority of the chapel is Early English from the time of the Hospitalers; the rest, including the font, belongs to the early 16th century.

In those early times the building we see

today would have served as chapel/hospital combined, serving the needs of a very small community. Other buildings would have existed — dwellings for the brethren and a farm.

The inside of the church is very austere, but nevertheless a few gems are to be found. The late Perpendicular font is of dark gritstone, octagonal in shape, each side with a shield bearing sacred, heraldic and other devices. This was a gift from Sir Thomas Pemberton, preceptor of Newland, under which Stydd was a camera (estate). The screen and pulpit are of very simple character, built of oak in the 17th century.

On the floor of the sanctuary are several grave slabs, the most interesting being that of Sir Adam and Lady Alicia de Cliderow of Salesbury Hall. The slab is damaged but the floreated design of a knight and his lady can be made out. The Cliderows were buried here around 1350.

Outside, in the old graveyard, stands an ancient cross base, thought to have come from Duddel Hill above Stydd.

The longer walk heads off for Hurst Green to return via Dutton Hall. For those who wish to return to Ribchester simply walk on down the lane, passing Stydd Almshouses, down to Stone Bridge to then turn right and follow the road into the village.

Stydd Chapel to Trough House

*Walk down the lane to gate near Almshouses and follow hedge to the left to go
over stiles and footbridge. Walk on to pass over stile and on along the
fence-line to pass over the stile onto road. Follow road to the left to pass over
stile by gate at Ease Barn Farm. Cross the field to riverbank via hedge stile.*

*We now follow the 'Ribble Way' that leads us to Dewhurst House then down
to the riverbank and on through the wooded wateredge to an open field via
stile. The way now goes over the hillside, over a stile and on up to pass through
a gateway near Hey Hurst. It now crosses the field to meet Heyhurst driveway
via stile. After passing over the stile opposite, the path leads down through the
fields to enter the farmyard at Trough House.*

Hey Hurst Farm

Hey Hurst Farmhouse is a delightfully pretty dwelling, built in the Jacobean
style, but I suspect it belongs to a later period. All the windows display cham-
fered mullions with drip moulds above, and the off-centred porch completes a
very fine picture indeed.

Trough House

Trough House takes its name from the old 'Trows Ferry', so named because
this curious craft resembled a pair of troughs or mangers lashed together that
was dragged by ropes or poles across the Ribble between Dinckley and Hurst
Green. Up to forty years ago a rowing boat was employed to ferry people across
the water. The last boat was replaced by a footbridge in the early 1950s.

TROUGH HOUSE

Remains of one of the ancient 'Trows' was found further down river at Salewheel; this is now on display in Blackburn Museum.

The house has a splendid frontage of mullioned windows with running hood-moulds above which, given their sharpness of style, means that the house was probably built in the late 17th century or later.

Standing above Trough House some way up the lane to Hurst Green is a south-facing bench that affords a good resting spot to sit and admire the valley.

Following the skyline from left to right we observe York, that tiny hamlet above Langho, then Cunliffe Hill, the site of early Celtic settlement. Next is Ramsgreave, once the ancient hunting forest for the Manor of Blackburn and finally the eye rests upon Mellor Hill, familiar long ago to both Roman and Celt.

The day we sat upon this bench we were treated to the sight of two roe deer strolling past. I hope you are as fortunate.

Trough House to Hurst Green

Follow the farm lane up to enter Hurst Green by the side of the Shireburn Arms.

The Old Village Cross, Hurst Green

The cross sits in the front garden of a house opposite the Shireburn Arms. Locals refer to it as a 'weeping cross' where funeral processions would stop to rest and drink.

The shaft is remarkably short suggesting that it may have been broken at one time and later re-inserted into the socket.

Hurst Green to Merrick's Hall

Walk up to the Shireburn Almshouses and turn down the lane opposite Smithy Row and at the end of the high hedge turn left and walk on to meet with a driveway. Pass through the white gate on the right and walk on past the converted mill to cross a footbridge on the side of the house. Walk up, noticing the lovely gardens and waterfalls down on the right, to enter field via stile.

Walk up the field to pass over stile and on to pass through farmyard onto roadway. Walk up the road to go left at footpath sign at Shire Lane House. Pass over stile and down the field to road via stile. Walk towards the church to turn down the farm lane on the right to Merrick's Hall.

MERRICK'S HALL

Merrick's Hall

Merrick's Hall (or Priest's House) was once a chantry priests' residence serving the chapel of St. John the Baptist at Bailey Hall. The south frontage is Georgian in style but the rear of the house is early 17th century — notice the mullioned and transomed window to the right of the front door. The interior preserves some of its earlier 16th century construction.

Carved upon one of the oaken beams is the following: ROBERTUS TAYLOR CANTORISTA HANC FABRICAM FECIT A.Dni M.D.XXIII. Robert Taylor was chaplain in 1517, and was still so in 1548 at 68 years of age. He was the last of the Bailey chantry priests having been presented to the benefice by Robert Cliderow of Mitton and instituted by Cardinal Wolsey. After the Dissolution, he lived on at his property in Waddington to the ripe age of 78. He is described to the last as "chaplain", but there is nothing further to connect him with Bailey.

The name Merrick's Hall comes from a family who had the freehold of this farm in the 18th century. A John Merrick of Bailey, a papist, registered an estate here in 1717.

Merrick's Hall to Bailey Hall

Pass through the farmyard into field and walk on (white posts) to enter the wooded ravine at Bailey Brook. The path now crosses the ravine by a footbridge and leads us up to the farmyard of Bailey Hall.

Bailey Hall and Chapel of St. John the Baptist

In the 13th century the manor of Bailey was held by Robert de Cliderow. His predecessor, Walter de Bailey, had in the latter part of the century come into possession of the manor of Stonyhurst, and had made that, instead of Bailey, the home of his family — soon to become the better-known family of Shireburn. From about 1293 Robert de Cliderow was a tonsured clerk in the King's Chancery, ordained in 1303 and destined to become parish priest of Wigan.

When he died he was buried at Salley Abbey and his tomb may still be seen in the abbey church. The brass effigy has gone but its matrix shows the outline of a figure clothed in amice and chasuble and wearing the tonsure and long flowing hair.

Round the margin runs the inscription in Lombardic capitals: +SIRE ROBERT DE CLYDERHOW PERSONE DE WYGAN GIST YCY DIEV DE SA ALME EYT VERRAY MERCY (1334). His estate in Bailey went then to his son Henry.

Robert's life was not without colour, reflecting the politics of the time. During the rebellion led by Thomas, Earl of Lancaster against Edward II and the Despensers (crushed by the defeat of Earl Thomas at Boroughbridge, March 1322, followed soon after by his execution), Robert was charged with having sent to the Earl at his own expense against the lord King two men-at-arms well mounted, to wit, Adam de Cliderow and John de Knoll, and with them four sturdy and valiant footmen armed with swords, knives, bows and arrows.

He was found guilty, committed to prison, released on bail for 10,000 marks (a mark was two thirds of a pound), and finally liberated on agreeing to pay a fine of £200.

The other incident was of the nature of a family quarrel with his kinsman and neighbour, Sir Adam de Cliderow of Salesbury. In 1332 Adam forcibly invaded the moated manor of Bailey and carried away all he could lay his hands on plus a number of articles evidently belonging to the chapel.

A trial was held at York in the summer of 1333, but we do not know the outcome of Robert's suit. Sir Adam was buried at Stydd Church, along with his wife, in 1337. Their mutilated sepulchral double incised slab can be seen in the church today.

After 1556 Bailey Hall was
sold to Shireburn of Stonyhurst
and was absorbed into their
manor. The house we see at
Bailey Hall today was built in
the latter half of the 16th century
upon the moated site of the
earlier hall. It is T-shaped with a
large number of mullioned windows, some with transom and
mouldings.

On the north side of the hall are the fenced-off remains of the 14th century
Chapel of St. John the Baptist. It was built by Robert de Cliderow in around
1325 as a chapel of ease to the mother church at Mitton and a chantry for the
Cliderows.

The remains of the chapel are very fragmentary, consisting of the lower
portions of the east wall with its diagonal angle buttresses and a portion of the
east end of the north wall. The diagram below shows a plan of what the chapel
would have looked like.

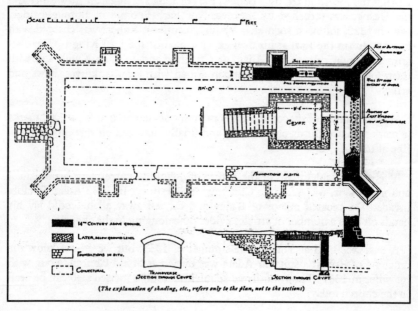

The odd projection on the east wall was a bell-cote, possibly a later addition. The east window, now built into the frontage of Stonyhurst College, is pointed with Y-intersecting tracery. The crypt is at the east end of the chapel below the sanctuary and stone steps lead down to a segmental brick barrel vault.

Near the north end of the east wall of the crypt at floor level is a drain connected to the moat. This burial vault is not part of the original chapel, and upon examining the brickwork I would assign it to the Elizabethan period, being built at the same time as the house and used by the Shireburn family whose only reference in the Mitton Church registers is a burial at Mitton in 1659.

The chapel and crypt were excavated in 1915, the bodies found being re-interred in consecrated ground. The chapel stood in a more or less complete state until 1730. The four walls stood until it was demolished by order of its owner, Mr Joseph Fenton of Rochdale, in the 1830s.

Bailey Hall to Dutton Hall

Pass through the farmyard and along the farm lane to a lone tree on the right. Walk into field on left and on past fence corner to pass over a footbridge. Cross the field on a left diagonal to enter Starling Brook ravine via stile. Walk down to cross footbridge and on up to farm lane via stile. Right, and walk on to Grindlestone House.

Pass rear of house and pass through the farmyard via gate and on to pass over corner stile. Pass over further stile to follow line of hedge on, over two stiles to pass over stile on left. Walk around the delf to pass over stile onto road. Walk down the road to turn right at Dutton Hall to view the frontage.

Dutton Hall

Standing high above Ribchester Bridge is the fine old residence of Dutton Hall, which claims a magnificent view from Wilpshire to Mellor.

The manor of Dutton was given in 1102 by Henry I to Robert de Lacy and from that time it became a member of the honor of Clitheroe. In 1290 it passed to Henry de Clayton of Clayton-le-Dale and descended regularly until 1400. The next principal family was the Towneleys, appearing about 1380. The present house was built by Richard Towneley around 1670 in the time of Charles II.

DUTTON HALL

The building consists of a hall with two cross wings with a splendid bay to the hall centre. The bay is square and overmighty, having seven-light transomed openings on both ground and first floors. The top of the bay has a balustrade with turned balusters, a good vantage spot on a fine summer's day. The stairwell and landing inside the hall was once used as the courtroom for the district. A small room off the staircase was used as a cell to secure offenders while awaiting trial.

Lower Dutton Cottages

This group of delightful 17th century cottages stand below Dutton Hall on Gallows Lane, so called after the gibbot that stood further up the lane at Three Turns. The local highwayman, Ned King, was displayed upon the gibbot having been tried and hanged for his crimes. Before his capture the unfortunate rogue is said to have sought refuge in the Punch Bowl Inn.

Dutton Hall to Stydd Almshouses

Pass through the field gate opposite the Hall front and on to pass through a gate by the round tank. Follow wall down to enter Duddel Wood via stile. Follow path down to the right to old mill lodge by footbridge — DO NOT GO OVER THIS BRIDGE. (The mill race on the right leads up to a stone built dam and beyond the lodge we can find the water wheel pit amidst the low ruins of the mill).

Walk downstream to cross lower footbridge and up to enter field via stile. Walk up to the left to go over stile by gate. Walk down the field, over stile by gate and on down to pass over bridge. The stream here is a man-made canal to divert various streams' waters to feed the mill that once stood at Stone Bridge. Walk over to the right to pass over stile by gate and on to go overe next stile. The path now leads us over a footbridge and then a stile and over to the right to pass over further stile. Walk up to the left to the Almshouses.

Stydd Almshouses

These attractive almshouses seem to have been built to catch the eye of all who pass down the narrow lane to Stydd.

They were endowed by John Shireburn in 1726 for five Roman Catholic widows or spinsters to dwell with free fuel and a small allowance. They are still maintained by the Catholic church and were fully modernised in 1990.

An open balustered stairway leads to an arcade supported by rustic Tuscan columns, all very curious and engaging. In the front garden is an open sided pitched-roof well to complete a delightful frontage.

Stydd to Ribchester

Walk down the lane to the main road at Stone Bridge. Follow the road to the right then left down back lane to find a streamside path that leads past the Roman Bath House to the riverbank near the Parish Church and Roman Museum.

Ribchester Village

The ancient village of Ribchester, built on the site of the Roman fort of Bremetennacum, holds many attractions for the visitor. Apart from the parish church, already cited, a visit to the Roman bath house and museum will prove enlightening.

The small museum, which stands at Churchgates, contains many of the finds discovered in the area. These include urns, coins, jewellery, monumental stones and so on and a replica of a ceremonial helmet, found at Ribchester, complete with mask and visor. The original, the finest of its type to be found in the Empire, is now in the British Museum.

On walking around the village, the careful eye will discover the remains of many 17th century buildings, the best example being a house of 1680 that stands along the road from the Black Bull to the river bank.

The 18th century is well represented with many fine handloom weavers' cottages, the best of which can be seen on Church Street to the front of the White Bull Hotel. Other loomshops can be found down from the Black Bull on Blackburn Road.

The Georgian period is

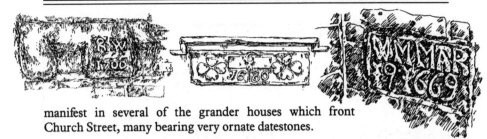

manifest in several of the grander houses which front Church Street, many bearing very ornate datestones.

With all this, along with good car parking facilities and a choice of good eating venues, Ribchester affords a great deal to the visitor and deserves a full day's exploration in itself.

CHURCHGATES, RIBCHESTER

White Bull, Ribchester

Standing in the village centre is the White Bull Inn, dated 1707. Its square middle projection is carried by pairs of Tuscan columns said to have come from the Roman fort, but this is very doubtful and early 18th century reproductions of this type can be found on the Shereburne Almshouses, in the parish church and astride the Roman road above Hothersall.

The inn was once used as the 'Court House' of Ribchester; surely no speaker would dry up from thirst. Apart from the datestone above, two others exist; on a spouting is cut I.A.I. 1747 (James and Jane Alston) and on the face of the stone step J.H.A. 1750 (John and Ann Hall). The "white bull" was carved long ago by a local hand and is Ribchester's proudest piece of sculpture, displaying workmanship worthy of Moore or Epstein.

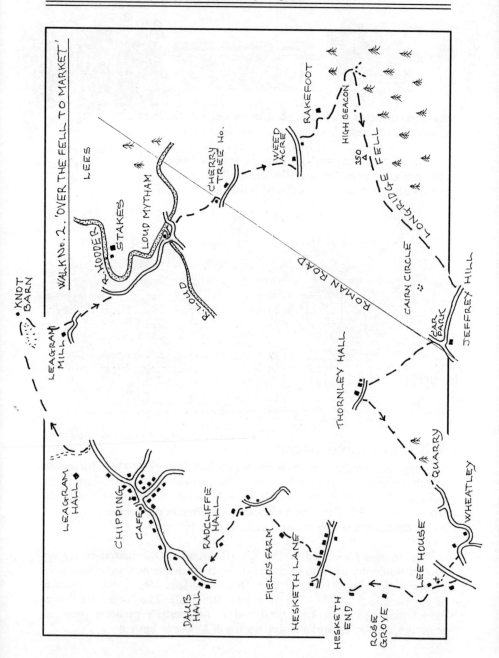

WALK No. 2. 'OVER THE FELL TO MARKET'

Walk 2

OVER THE FELL TO MARKET

*Longridge Fell, Hesketh Lane, Chipping
and Loud Mytham*

12½ miles, 6 hours

MAP: *O.S. sheets SD 64/74 & 63/73 PATHFINDER*

LUNCH: *Sun Inn or Cobble Corner Cafe, Chipping*

START: *Jeffrey Hill Car Park, Longridge Fell*

Today we start our walk from Britain's most southerly named 'fell' to descend into the Vale of the Loud to visit a once ancient market town. The return is via Loud Mytham with an ascent of the eastern section of Longridge Fell.

In between we shall visit many places of fascinating historical and architectural interest. With contrasting landscapes and splendid views this walk makes for a wonderful day out.

Cairn Circle, Longridge Fell (SD 645405)

The OS Index records an ancient Cairn Circle near the summit of Thornley Hall Fell, a few hundred yards north-east of Jeffrey Hill car park. The site is marked by a cairn of stones of recent origin. The cairn in question is a paved circular feature of loose stones about 30ft. in diameter mostly covered by heather. The circle is comparable to the cairn circle on Chetham Close, Turton, that has been defined as a roundhouse of Bronze Age origin.

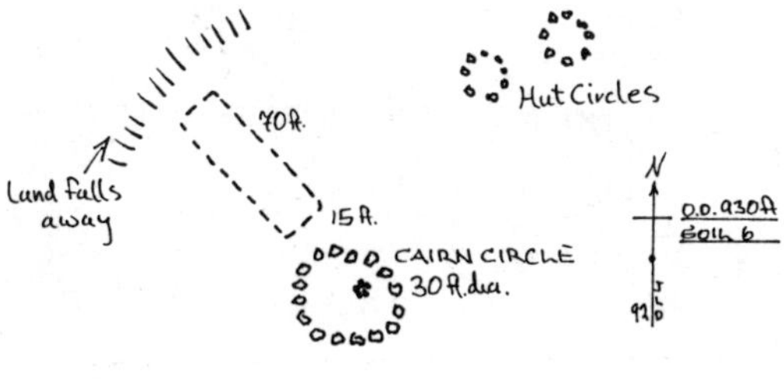

Below the cairn, to the north-west, is a rectangular feature 70ft. by 15ft. being most marked to the north. There may have been a portal where the land falls away. There are also slight remains of circular structures to the north-east of the cairn circle which may be hut sites. There may be a further hut circle/tumulus deep in the ling about 100 yards north-east of the cairn circle.

The Roman Road from Ribchester to Overborrow makes a major north-east turn at Jeffrey Hill and some suppose that a Roman signal station would have stood nearby.

Jeffrey Hill Car Park to Thornley Hall

Walk down the road passing the David Procter Bench, that allows one to reflect on the distant Bowland Fells, for a short way to pass over stile on left. Walk on down the field (passing over the Roman road), past the trees to follow the fence down to the roadway at Thornley Hall via gate.

Thornley Hall

Thornley, or Patten Hall is a plain building, much modernised, but retaining some ancient features.

Over the doorway is the inscription 'B.O. MICHAEL DOUGHTIE 1605', and in the dining room over the mantlepiece is a small cupboard on which are the initials of Elizabeth and Mary Patten and the date 1709.

The house is named after Elizabeth Stanley, daughter of Thomas Patten of Preston and mother of Sir Edward Stanley of Bickerstaffe, Earl of Derby.

Thornley Hall

On the road west from Thornley Hall, set in the hedge, can be found the old village stocks of Thornley-with-Wheatley. Wheatley, 'Watelei', is noted in the Norman Survey of 1086 as a manor.

On the boundary of Thornley-with-Wheatley and Dutton is a stone called 'The White Stoop' and a group of stones called 'Cripple Oak'.

Thornley Hall to Lee House Chapel

Walk down the road a short way to leave by track going down to stream and walk on round to enter hedge-lined old lane. Follow the lane on to meet with farm lane. Right, walk along the lane to roadway and continue directly on to Wheatley Farm (RHA 1774). Walk down the road, right at junction, past the corner cottage to pass over stile on right. Cross the field to roadway at Lee House via hedge stile.

LEE HOUSE

Lee House Chapel

The Roman Catholic church of St. William of York, also known as Lee House Chapel, is a good example of a post-Reformation chapel. The chapel was founded by Thomas Eccles of Thornley in 1738 and was originally housed in the present priest's house. A secret room built into the eaves of the building can still be located. This house has a datestone of 1677, with the initials T.A., and at the rear a few old mullioned windows still exist.

Thomas Eccles gave the house to the English Franciscans, and on their approaching extinction in 1859 the secular clergy took charge for a time. After 1859 it was served by the English Benedictines, whose gravestones can be found in the churchyard.

Standing in the churchyard is a very fine reproduction of a Celtic High Cross to the memory of the late Father Moloney, died 1988. The cross is set into the pedestal of the ancient Wheatley Lane Cross that once stood near to Wheatley Brook. For years the base was hidden in the undergrowth of the graveyard. Its present position and use is a wonderful tribute to a very fine and well loved man.

Lee House to Hesketh End

Come out onto the main road, right and on to go right again up farm lane. Walk on to pass through gate at second farmyard. Continue on to enclosure to pass through wooden gate on right. Follow right-hand hedge on to pass through lower gateway and cross the field to pass over stile onto farm lane. Pass over footbridge on right and cross the field to Hesketh End Farm via gate.

Hesketh End

HESKETH END

Richard Alston built this house on land purchased from Gabrial Hesketh, a recent landowner in the district. The building comes to note by the fact that it has a running frieze of two line panels forming a band of lettering around the house. The inscriptions contained in the frieze refer to events in English history from the Roman period to the Battle of Flodden Field in 1513.

In 1907 the house was thoroughly restored after a fire, the main front being largely reconstructed. The original building probably extended further. The inscription runs across the front wall in double lines, carved on six separate stones.

The wording on each stone is complete in itself, except in the last two stones, and is as follows:

1. BRUTUS ERECTUS LON DINV ANTE CHRIST 1108
2. CESAR CONQVERT AN GLIA ANTE CHRIST 58
3. SAXONII CONQVERT ANGLIA ANNO DON 447 EBISCOPAT IB
4. DANII CONQVERT ANGLIA ANNO DON 1018
5. ANGLIA IN CO M**SIVE**SHIRI
6. ANGL** RECEP* FIDM AD 179

This is continued on four stones along the return of the west wing:

1. ANNO DOMI 1591 ELIS REGI REGNO ANNI ETATIS NOSTRE
2. ROBART ALSTUN 25 RIC ALSTUN IVNIOR 5
3. A CREACIONE MUNDI 5553 A CONQVES TO ANGLIE 524 DEUM TIME REGEM HONOR
4. RESPICE FINEM ET NVNQV AM PECCABIS PROXIMUM AMA

Hesketh End

To the left of this last stone is another stone with the name of RICHARDE ALSTUN 53. On the main south front are other inscribed stones, one with the sacred monogram between two crosses, another with the fragment RIC AULSTU, and a third ALSTUN HATH INHERITED HERE IB 18 YER. The west wall retains its old rough stone walling unrestored. The chimney has two gargoyles in the angles. There is an inscribed stone in the main bedroom — FEAR GOD AND LOVE THE RIGHT.

What a sense of wonder the local peasantry must have felt when looking upon the house of Richard Alston, a ray of illumination in their dark rustic lives.

The cottage beyond Hesketh End is known as Chalk Hall, once the home of one Captain Alston. The doorhead is dated 1626 with the initials of Richard Alston and the arms of Alston.

One of the area's many fine inns stands across the way at Hesketh End. The Dog and Partridge (known as the Green Man in the 17th century and Cliviger House before 1630) was the source of a noted 18th century play. The drama entitled "Kelly, Or the Modern Reformer" was the work of Peter Walkden a Mancunian diarist and Presbyterian minister who lived at Daub Hall near Chipping.

Walkden was the incumbent of the Hesketh Lane Independent Chapel from 1711 to 1738. The chapel, now Chapel House, was one of the earliest non-conformist places of worship in Lancashire. The doorhead bears a date 1705.

Hesketh End to Hesketh Lane

Pass through the stock-pen gates on the right of farmyard entrance and walk on to Chalk Hall (1626) via gate. Pass the front of house, over stile and along the paved path to the roadway at Hesketh Lane.

Hesketh Lane to Chipping via Daub Hall

Pass over wall-stile at Maycroft House, through gate and on to go over ladder fence-stile. Walk down to the right to pass through white gate and on along hedge on left to pass over ladder-stile in hedge by gate (notice the old stone clam bridge). Walk up the field, over stile and on to enter farmyard via gate. Pass house front to go over fence-stile and on over the field to pass over corner stile. Walk to the right to go over clam bridge and on to the road via hedge-stile.

Left and on to enter lane at corner and on to go left after Radcliffe Cottage. Follow lane to Radcliffe Hall. Pass over wall-stile between garage and water trough and walk up to the left to pass over two stiles. Follow hedgerow up to road via stiles. Daub Hall is just down to the left. For Chipping follow the road to the right to the Cobble Corner Cafe (signed copies of our books available here, plus excellent fare).

Daub Hall

Daub Hall

Daub Hall is first recorded in 1334, when John, son of William de Dubhill, was registered as living in the parish of Chipping. The place-name comes from the Old English 'dub', meaning pool, or, in this case, ditch.

The Singleton family dwelt here from 1578 to 1682 when the hall passed to the Parkinson family. From 1725 to 1736, Peter Walkden, a Manchester diarist and incumbent of the Hesketh Lane Independent Chapel from 1711 to 1738, had lease of the property from John Parkinson.

Whilst in Chipping, Walkden wrote a drama entitled "Kelly, Or the Modern Reformer" based on behaviour he observed among those who frequented the Dog and Partridge (formerly the Grean Man and Cliviger House in the 17th century). The play is a gem in its own right and ought to be performed again.

DAUB HALL

An old doorhead is built into the right side of the house front. It is dated 1707 with the initials L.W., being those of Lawrence Wall of Preston who built the house. His son married a Mary Parkinson. Signs of the house's older mullioned windows can still be made out, along with the massive weight of a cheese press.

Chipping

The delightful village of Chipping and its surroundings are fully described in Volume 8 of the BRIGANTIA series, 'The Forest of Bowland'.

Chipping to Loud Mytham

Walk on past the church to go down Talbot Street to go left at the War Memorial. Walk along the road, past the Lodge House, to go left up Leagram Hall driveway to just below the entrance to the Hall proper. Walk directly over the field on your right to pass over fence-stile. On, following line of fence to go over next stile. Walk on to cross stream and up to pass over stile. Continue on, over stile and on to go over footbridge in a delightful wooded glen (notice the old Leagram Mill mill-race running at a higher level than the stream).

Walk on and up to the left to pass over stile. Cross the field directly to Knott Hill quarry and limekiln. Follow the lane to the right to the roadway at Leagram Mill (now a private house). Pass over the stile opposite and follow the hedgerow down to pass over stile onto road. Right, walk along the road to Loud Mytham Bridge.

Loud Mytham Hall

Loud Mytham is a large two-storey yeoman farmhouse of the 17th century.

During the 16th century a branch of the old Catholic family of Crombleholme lived here. In 1534 Edward Crombleholme was paid 26s. 8d. for making 160 roods of paling, to be placed above Leagram deer park foss (ditch).

Edward is also recorded as felling oak trees in a place above Wardsley called Aklaye, the 'ack' or 'oak' being a reminder of the forest which used to be there.

The Crombleholmes were followed by the Marsdens from around 1620 to 1720. They in turn were followed by the Slater family.

An account is preserved by the Slater family of 'two rebel officers calling at their house' of Loudmytholme, after the retreat from Derby in the Jacobite rising of 1745, asking for shelter and 'to be directed to the King's Road' to Lancaster.

Many people in the area supported the Jacobite cause, and in Chaigley there are the remains of a barracks in which soldiers were stationed in order to quell any insurgency within the district.

The Stonyhurst Magazine of July 1885 gives the following account: "The country was laid under Martial Law. The luckless insurgents were hunted like wolves amid the neighbouring hills of Preston, and small troops of Hanoverian soldiers were posted throughout the country in bands, and vigorously enforced their presence on the Lancashire peasants, who cherished a faithful devotion to the unfortunate exiles.

"At Chaigley, one of these barracks was established. It is now in ruins, roofless, dilapidated, ivy-grown, and is still pointed out as the seat whence the soldiery sallied forth to harass the lands and humble abodes of the outlaws."

Loud Mytham to Longridge Fell Trig. Point

Cross the bridge and follow the road to the left, up to go over stile on right. Contour over to the left to pass over footbridge. Follow stream and hedgerow up to meet with farm lane (Roman road) via gate on left of barn. Pass barn and walk on to road via gate.

Left, walk along the road passing Cherry Tree House, on down to pass through gate on right at footpath sign. Walk up the field to pass over stile by hedgerow tree. Continue on up the field and then over to the right to meet with road via gate. Left, walk on to go up Rake Foot Farm driveway (B & B) to go over stile by higher cattle grid. Pass over other stile on left and walk up the field to enter the rake (sunken track leading diagonally up the fell). Walk up the rake to fork in path near summit ridge.

Take the right-hand path and after a few yards leave by a small path on the right that leads through the conifers to an enchanted grove of pines. Follow the path on and along the wallside to pass over fence-stile and on along the track to the summit Trig. Pt.

Longridge Fell

Longridge Fell is the most southerly named fell in England. A walk along this isolated fell never disappoints — the Bowland massif laid out in all its glory, deep folds leading the walker's eye on to further journeys of exploration, and all around the green heartland of Lancashire lying below the western Pennines and spreading out to the Irish Sea. A joy to behold.

Longridge Fell Summit to Jeffrey Hill Car Park

Follow the wallside path on to the road. Walk up and over the brow to the car park.

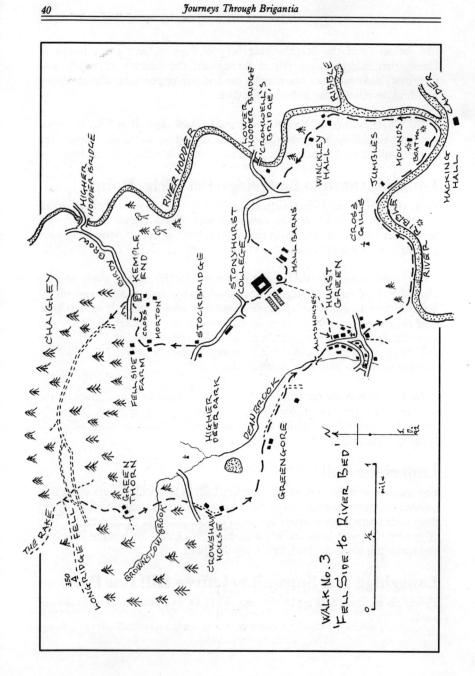

WALK No. 3
'Fell Side to River Bed'

16/10/94 (2 Seperate Walks)

Walk 3

FELL SIDE TO RIVER BED

Longridge Fell, Hurst Green,
Hacking Boat & Stonyhurst

11 miles, 6 hours
or two shorter walks of 7 & 5 miles

MAP: *O.S. sheets SD 64/74 & 63/73 PATHFINDER*

LUNCH: *Bailey Arms, Hurst Green*

START: *Kemple End parking area or Hurst Green.*

This walk allows us to gain an acquaintance with the higher and lower former
deer parks of Stonyhurst, once hunting grounds of the Shireburns. I, for one,
always start this walk from Kemple End allowing me to look over the Ribble
Valley and take in the classic view of Pendle, then after a delightful forest
stroll gain a magnificent picture of the Bowland Fells from the Rake top.

History and scenery meet us at every turn, making for the perfect day out
between fell side and river bed.

Kemple End Parking Area to Top of Rake

Pass through the gate opposite and follow the path above the old quarry and on
following wall up to meet with forest road. Walk up the road (good views of
Pendle and the Ribble Valley) for some way to go left at junction and on to
meet with bridleway. Follow bridleway up to the right through the trees, across
higher track and on to meet with 'The Rake' track (fine views here over the
Bowland Fells with Ingleborough and Pen-y-Ghent in the distance).

Top of Rake, Longridge Fell

This is one of my best loved spots and many's the time that I have sat to have a
brew and a smoke by the little cairn of stones looking through the canopy of
pines to the Bowland Fells beyond — wonderful.

Longridge Fell is the most southerly named fell in Britain. It affords many fine views over the surrounding area and is blessed with many paths for one to explore its length.

Rake Top to Crowshaw House

Follow track to the left (southwards) to join with forest road and on down to lower roadway. Walk to the left then follow path down to the right to west of Green Thorn Farm. Continue on down fence-side path, past stile and on to cross Brownslow Brook. Walk on through the forest to the main road. Walk to the right then left down the farm drive to Crowshaw House.

Crowshaw House

Crowshaw was part of the estate of the Clitherocs of Bailey. During the Civil Wars it was tenanted by Richard Holden, younger brother of John Holden of Chaigley, probably the recusant (one who held the Roman Catholic faith) of that name who had his lands sequestered by the Commonwealth of Oliver Cromwell.

This spot gains its notoriety from an incident that illustrates the turbulence of those times. A priest, discovered in the act of saying the mass at Chapel House Farm in Chaigley, was summarily executed there. His severed head was flung over a fence where a Mrs Holden of Crowshaw House redeemed it, gathering it up into her apron and smuggling it into her home.

The head and other chapel trappings — missal, cloth, vestments and candles — were concealed and preserved as relics by the family. These were kept in great secrecy at Crowshaw until the establishment of the Jesuits at Stonyhurst when the relics could be then shown. In 1887 they were in the possession of the Holdens of Hill House, Woodplumpton, and an elaborate description was printed in the 'Stonyhurst Magazine', November 1887.

Crowshaw House to Greengore

Follow track to pass over stile by gate and on down the track to Greengore.

Greengore

GREENGORE

Standing on the side of an old moorland trackway is the imposingly strange house of Greengore. Mention of the house was first recorded in 1314 when 'Thomas de Greengore confirmed to Adam his son, certain land in Bailey, excepting the Greengore'. During the 16th and 17th centuries, the house was used as a hunting lodge for the Stonyhurst Deer Park and is said to have played host to the Lancastrian Kings.

The huge buttresses point to the great age of the building, these being a later addition because the house was originally built of a single stone wall, rendering poor support. The windows are Elizabethan, allowing the interior to be well-lighted for the period.

The name Greengore means 'green mud', suggesting that the land was very marshy in bygone times.

Greengore Camping Barn

By the side of the main house is a recently established Camping Barn. Sleeping accommodation for 12 persons is on the upper floor and a toilet is in another building close by. There are three hot plates for cooking and two electric heaters on a coin meter. A small drying room and an outdoor barbecue are provided. Cars can be parked in the farmyard.

I have visited the barn myself and highly recommend it. Bookings: Bowland Barns Reservation Office, 16 Shawbridge Street, Clitheroe BB7 1LY. Tel: (0200) 28366 (24 hour answer service).

Greengore to Hurst Green

Continue on down the farm lane, left at the junction and on to cross Dean Brook Bridge. Follow track on to the Almshouses at Hurst Green.

Shireburn Almshouses

"A rolling stone gathers no moss" the saying goes, but when the almshouses 'rolled' from Longridge Fell they gained a top storey.

The almshouses were built in 1706 by Sir Nicholas Shireburn and were originally sited on the east end of Longridge Fell.

They consisted then of ten rooms and a chapel, with names over the doors of the villages from which the poor of Shireburn's lands were drawn: Aighton, Bailey, Chaigley, Dutton, Ribchester, Wiswell and Mitton. In 1946 the Almshouses were dismantled and rebuilt as workers' cottages at the College gates in Hurst Green.

The plan is an adaptation of the usual courtyard type employed in such institutions, combined with an E-shaped house plan. The middle part of the main block was originally intended for the chapel but has never been used as such.

In reality, the courtyard is a raised terrace approached by a stone balustrade with turned balusters. In the pediment (triangular low-pitched gable end of a 'Greek' temple-like building) are the arms of Shireburn with crest and supporters and below, in large letters, 'Shireburn Almshouses'.

Hurst Green to Hacking Boat House

Walk down by the left of the Shireburn Arms to pass over stile by gate (we now follow the 'Ribble Way'). Walk down by the hedge, over stream and on down to pass over stile and footbridge. Walk up to the left to pass over stile and on down to pass over footbridge. Follow riverside path on passing Jumbles Farm to the derelict Boat House.

JUMBLES

Jumbles

On your way round to Jumbles Farm you may have noticed a stone cross squatting on the summit of a sharp hill south-east of Hurst Green. This is the Delph or Gills Cross, an ancient pedestal surmounted by an ornate 19th century cross shaft. The cross originally stood by the main road above the farm and was then known as Cross Kells.

Jumbles is built in the late Stewart style. A dated tablet to the side of the front door informs us that the house was built by John Hill and Richard, his son, in 1723. To the right of the doorway stand the remains of an old cheese press.

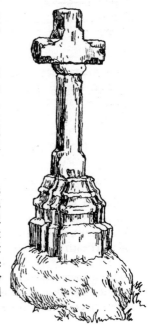

The house takes its name from Jumbles Rocks, an ancient and hazardous fording point on the river that links the two Bronze Age sites of Winckley Lowes and Brockhall Eases.

The Bronze Age Mounds

Two large mounds stand near to the boat house, both of which are man-made. The one by the nearby barn was excavated by Rev. J. R. Luck of Stonyhurst College in 1894. The tumulus revealed a cinerary urn of c. 1250 B.C. which contained the cremated remains of a body. Also found were a young man's skull and a flint knife, a boy's skull and a child's skull.

The burial is one of an important person — probably some local chieftain — buried near the ancient natural ford at Jumbles Rocks which must have been known and used by early man even in Neolithic times.

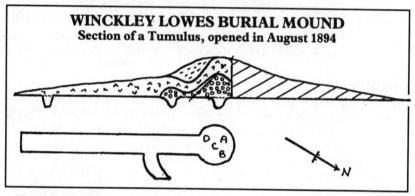

WINCKLEY LOWES BURIAL MOUND
Section of a Tumulus, opened in August 1894

The second, larger, mound is known as Loe Hill and has only recently been declared man-made. No major excavation work has been carried out on the mound and its purpose remains uncertain.

Some suppose that it was built after the Battle of Billington in A.D. 798; towards the close of the 8th century the Anglo-British kingdom of Northumbria was fraught with internal conflict.

In 774 the Northumbrians drove their King, Alhred, from York and took Aethelred, son of Moll, to be their lord. Aethelred reigned for four years, being driven from his kingdom in the revolt of 778 which was led by Aethelred and Heardberht, who instated Aelfwald as their lord. The year 789 saw the downfall and death of Aelfwald who was slain by Sicga.

His nephew, Osred, son of Alhred, succeeded to the kingdom. The following year Osred was betrayed and driven out of Northumbria and Aethelred returned again to his kingdom. In 794 Aethelred was killed by his own court and, after many months of anarchy and savage Viking raids, Eardwulf succeeded to the perilous and unstable dignity of the Northumbrian Crown.

In 798, a rival faction had gathered strength and was prepared to contest the government of the kingdom with Eardwulf. The decisive battle between the King and the would-be usurpers took place hereabouts in that same year. The chiefs of this conspiracy were Wada and Alric, son of Heardberht, both implicated in a former rebellion which ended in the deposition and death of the previous king, Aethelred. Simeon of Durham gives an account of the battle:

"A confederacy was made of the murderers of King Aethelred; Wada, chief in that conspiracy, with his force went against Eardwulf, in a place called by the English Billangahoh (Billington), near Walalege (Whalley), and on either side many were slain; Wada, the chief, with his men, was put to flight, and King Eardwulf regally achieved victory over the enemies."

The Anglo-Saxon Chronicle for that year states:

"In this year in Spring, on 2nd April, there was a great battle at Whalley in Northumbria, and there was slain Alric, son of Heardberht, and many others with him."

A third mound once stood across the river at Brockhall Eases. During the summer of 1836 Thomas Hubbersty, the farmer at Brockhall, was removing a large mound of earth when he discovered a stone-lined cist. This was said to contain human bones and the rusty remains of some spearheads of iron. The whole crumbled to dust on exposure to air. Given that the spearheads were made of iron, one is tempted to describe it as a 1st millenium B.C. burial.

Stone-lined cists are known in the Iron Age but these are invariably surface graves. Barrow inhumations of this type have been found in Scotland, though such mounds are cairns and not mounds of earth. Again, whilst primary inhumations in barrows are not uncommon in the post-Roman period, stone-lined cists are very rare. Only one site, Chelmorton in Derbyshire, has been recorded in the north of England.

It is also possible to see the mound as a Bronze Age earthen bowl-barrow; consequently, one could put the barrow into the wider pattern of Bronze Age settlement in the area. Its close proximity to Winckley Lowe might indicate that the site had some ritual significance. Given the lack of dateable remains the site must remain the subject of speculation.

Hacking Boat House

The old Boat House stands as a reminder of the days when a ferry transported travellers and wanderers alike across the waters between Hacking and Winckley. A few years ago the old boat was found in a barn standing near to the house and was taken away to be restored. It now stands on display in Clitheroe Castle Museum.

In times past a bell was mounted upon a pole on the Hacking bank of the river. This acted as a signal to the ferryman requesting his or her — the last ferryman was a woman — services.

On the opposite bank of the river stands the magnificent Jacobean mansion of Hacking Hall, resplendent with its many mullioned gabled frontage.

Boat House to Winckley Hall Farm

Follow riverside path on and into the farmyard.

Winckley Hall

Winckley Hall was part of the Knights Hospitallers estate in Aighton and Bailey which was treated as part of their manor at Stydd. The old hall, now Winckley Hall Farm, displays little of its Elizabethan origins.

The central gabled section is the oldest part of the house and to the rear can be seen two splendid mullioned and transomed windows with hood moulding above. Also at the rear is a 'Donkey Walk' or 'Horse-gin', complete with its old grinding stones. This was used for grinding corn up till the late 19th century.

The most notable occupant of Winckley Hall was Dorothy Winckley who, through marriage, moved to Pleasington Hall, near Blackburn. She married first a Southworth, then a de Hoghton, and finally Thomas Ainsworth. It is claimed that she is the 'White Lady' who wanders the lanes around the Great Hall at Samlesbury.

An ancient cross once stood in the grounds of Winckley Hall in an elevated position at the top of Spring Wood overlooking the River Hodder. In 1928 the entire cross, including the pedestal and plinth, was removed and it now stands as a headstone of a grave in Great Mitton churchyard — a memorial to Hartley Baldwin of Winckley Hall.

The barn at the farm is worth looking at being a magnificent example of an aisled building. By adding aisles on one or both sides and on one or both ends, this method of building was useful for increasing the floor area of a hall or barn.

Upon leaving the farmyard, notice the duck ponds. These are the remains of a moat that once surrounded Winckley Hall on all sides.

The place-name 'Winckley' is of Celtic origin — vindo (white) kaito (wood) in Old Welsh — gwyn coed meaning "the glade in the white wood."

Lower Hodder Bridge

Standing slightly down river from Lower Hodder Bridge is the remains of the 16th century Old Hodder Bridge, known locally as Cromwell's Bridge. This name is derived from the likely crossing by Oliver Cromwell at this point on the eve of the Battle of Preston in 1648.

The bridge was built by Sir Richard Shireburn in 1562 at a cost of £70. In 1569 a collection was made in the Blackburn Hundred towards further building work on the bridge. Across the bridge, on the Mitton Magna side, stands an old milestone of 1766 erected by John Shireburn. "To Lancafter 16M. To Whalley M 3. I:S 1766".

Many strange objects adorn the farmsteads of the Lower Hodder. Two stone heads and an old font of 1710 are but a few. The stone heads are included in a study of Lancashire Stone and Celtic Heads by Alice Smith of Copster Green, from which the following information is taken.

The head on the right is finely carved from sandstone, showing a male with long flowing hair and a fine beard on the chin; around the neck he wears a ruff.

The other is very grand showing Classical influences. The headgear seems Eastern or mediaeval, the beard and moustache long and flowing. This head was dug up by a gardener who lived on the south side of Jeffrey Hill who sold it to a man who lived nearby.

Winckley Hall to Stonyhurst College

Pass through the farmyard and up the lane to pass through kissing gate opposite 'new' Winckley Hall. Walk on to pass through next gate and on and down to the road via stiles. Walk up the road opposite and at Stonyhurst village turn right down Hall Barns drive. Walk past the rear of the barn to college lane. Follow lane to the right to the front of the College.

Woodfields

Woodfields is a converted 17th century house which is now dated 1813, with the initials N.C.A. Four cottages across the way also carry these initials with a date of 1810.

The earlier parts of the house can be seen on the side of the present house, once the original frontage. Two mullioned windows and a string mould attest to its early foundations.

The Hall Barns

Though stone is the predominant material, inside the Hall Great Barn five enormous cruck-trusses dominate the pile. Built of timber felled in the Forest of Bowland, the barn illustrates just how fine the oak once was here.

Stonyhurst College

The most prominent house in the Ribble Valley is without doubt that of Stonyhurst. It was the main residence of the Shireburn family until 1794 when it was placed at the disposal of the Jesuit Fathers of Liege. Today it is one of the finest Roman Catholic boarding schools for boys in the country.

Land known as 'the Stonyhurst' was granted before 1209 by Hugh, son of John de Mitton to Ellis, son of Alexander de Winckley. An oratory was built here by John de Bailey in 1372, remains of which were discovered in 1856 when pulling down the buildings known as 'Sparrows Hall', the old infirmary, which stood near the north-east corner of the quadrangle.

An eye witness at the time is quoted as saying: 'When the ceiling was pulled down an oaken roof was laid bare, the spandrils of every panel being carved with roses.' These spandrils were found to be of the same design and workmanship as those in the roof of Mitton Church, showing that they had been built in the time of Edward III.

The building we see today was started by Hugh Shireburne in about 1523, the major part being the work of Sir Richard Shireburn who began work with the gatehouse in 1592. Additions and alterations, especially in the gardens, were made by Sir Nicholas Shireburn who inherited in 1690. His daughter and heir, the Duchess of Norfolk, made a few further alterations, one of which was to bring the Bailey Chapel east window to be incorporated into the frontage.

Stonyhurst contains many priceless treasures, the oldest being a 7th century copy of St. John's Gospel which belonged to St. Cuthbert, a relic from his tomb in Durham Cathedral opened in 1827. The binding of the book is the finest example of Anglo-British leatherwork to survive from that period.

Strangely, Stonyhurst overlooks Mellor Hill, one of the few places that Cuthbert's body was rested in the 9th century in order to establish a church there.

Another treasure is the cope of Henry II, left by that monarch in his will to Westminster Abbey and later used by Henry VIII at the Field of the Cloth of Gold. Also housed are the embroidered cap of Sir Thomas More and Queen Catherine of Aragon's chasuble and dalmatics.

During the Civil Wars, General Oliver Cromwell stayed at Stonyhurst overnight after a forced march from Knaresborough. He arrived on the 16th August 1648 with 8,500 men who encamped within the deer park.

Cromwell is said to have slept upon a table, now known as 'Oliver Cromwell's Table', with pistol and sword at his side. It was thought that he was only too wary of assassination, for the Shireburns were well known Papists. The likeliest derivation of the legend, however, is that Cromwell simply dozed off at the table after dinner and after writing despatches, rather than his choosing the table as a bed for the night!

Early the following morning he marched his army the length of Longridge Fell to meet the Scottish Army under James, Duke of Hamilton. They met north of Preston on Ribbleton Moor. The encounter is known to history as the Battle of Preston, though the last action was actually fought on Warrington Bridge.

Stonyhurst to Kemple End

Walk on past the front of the college on up to roadway. Take the road up, passing Stockbridge Cottages, to a cottage on the right at Stock Bridge. Pass through gate at side rear of cottage and follow the stream up to pass over stile by gate. Continue on up, over stile and through Fell Side farmyard to pass over fence-stile over on the right.

Cross field directly to pass over stile by corner of wood. Follow wall on to pass over stile on right of gate. Walk round and back up to view Kemple End Cross. Follow edge of wood on to pass through gate onto parking area.

Kemple End

At Kemple End only a cluster of houses remain of the once village of Morton, recorded in 1276 when Almarica, daughter of Sinward de Morton and Aighton, complained of disseisin of the free tenement in Morton and Aighton (Oak Town) by Godith de Riddings and others (Rydding's Farm stands below Kemple End above the Hodder).

To the south-west of Morton House is an old well, known as 'Doctors Well'.

Another old settlement recorded in 1246 was Daniscole (David's Hut), an Old Norse settlement. This settlement, later known as 'Dandy Row', stood on the site of Nooks Farm to the west of Kemple End.

The cross in the field above Morton House is known as the 'Paulinus or Kemple End Cross'. The monument consists of a short, thick cross, roughly cut out of coarse sandstone, mortised into a huge block of stone which is set upon other large stones almost level with the ground.

For those with an interest in Lay Lines, the cross stands on the Belenos Line which also cuts through Glastonbury Tor, the most significant Lay Line in Britain.

Belenos was a god of the Celts whose festival, Baltain, took place on 1st May.

The name means 'a goodly fire' and the festival was connected with the promotion of fertility, and was much concerned with magical rites to encourage the growth of cattle and crops.

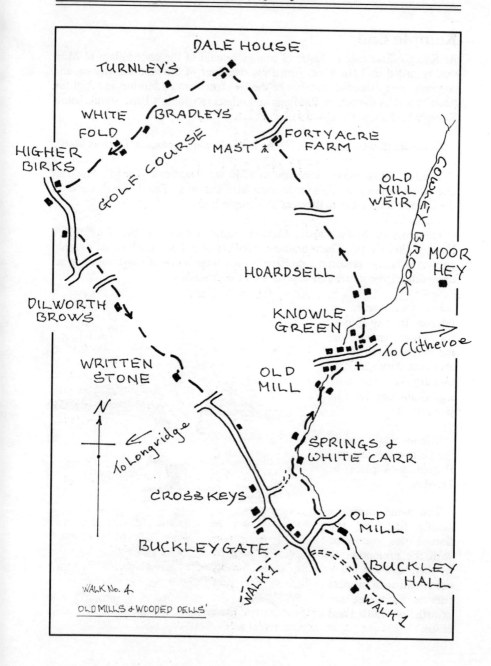

DALE HOUSE

TURNLEY'S

WHITE FOLD · BRADLEYS

HIGHER BIRKS

GOLF COURSE

MAST · FORTYACRE FARM

OLD MILL WEIR

COWLEY BROOK

MOOR HEY

HOARDSELL

KNOWLE GREEN

To Clithevoe

DILWORTH BROWS

WRITTEN STONE

OLD MILL

N

To Longridge

SPRINGS & WHITE CARR

CROSS KEYS

OLD MILL

BUCKLEY GATE

WALK 1

BUCKLEY HALL

WALK 1

WALK No. 4

'OLD MILLS & WOODED DELLS'

Walk 4

OLD MILLS
AND
WOODED DELLS

*Buckley Gate, Knowle Green, Higher Birks
and Written Stone*

5½ miles, 2½ hours

MAP: *O.S. sheet SD 63/73 PATHFINDER*

LUNCH: *Cross Keys, Buckley Gate*

START: *Cross Keys, Buckley Gate*

This walk can be linked with the western section of Walk One to make for a full day out.

The south-eastern slopes of Longridge Fell provide a watershed to several streams which all flow down to meet the Ribble. The ravines the streams have cut are bounded by little known paths that are idyllic places to wander, through wooded glens with waterfalls, weirs and ruins.

One such stream we follow today: Cowley Brook (Boyce's Brook) which rises on the fell above Knowle Green and makes its way through Dilworth Bottoms and Buckley Woods to the Ribble at Ribchester.

Today these are peaceful places but once they were alive with industry and worker folk. At one time there were eight water powered mills by Cowley Brook. Starting from the fell source we had Moor Hey Bobbin Mill, Knowle Green Spinning Mill, Knowle Green Foundry, Clay Hill Bobbin Mill, Lum Mill, White Carr Bobbin Mill, Cage Mill and Ribchester Bobbin Mill.

Add to all this a glimpse of the Vale of the Loud and a visit to the Written Stone and we have all the ingredients for a delightful day out.

BAILEY HOUSE

Buckley Gate

Buckley is first mentioned in a 13th century grant by William Moton to Thomas, son of Ralph de Ribchester. Two ancient crosses once stood in Buckley, one near the Cross Keys Inn, the other near Higher Alston.

At Buckley Gate stands a fine 17th century farmhouse known as Bailey House.

Cross Keys, Buckley Gate, to White Carr

Walk down the Ribchester road, passing Greenmoor Lane, to go down the farm lane on the left to go over stile on left at entry to Buckley Hall. Walk down the field on a sharp left diagonal to enter Cage Mill by stile at rear of house and walk up the driveway to the road. Walk to the right to pass over stile by gate on left. Follow hedgerow/stream on, over stile and on to go over footbridge. Follow fence on left to pass through gate to White Carr.

White Carr and the Old Mills

This stretch of walk up to Knowle Green must rate as one of the most picturesque within the district. Of interest here are the remains of the area's old mills; one, Cage, has been tastefully converted into a modern dwelling, but one can still observe the original layout.

Below Knowle Green a deserted mill stands in melancholy decay amid a forlorn glen shaded by a mass of varied leafage, throwing an air of enchantment and mystery over the place.

WHITE CARR

At the foot of the glen stands White Carr ford and farm, with its old water pump that once brought forth the cool waters from the underground depths. All in all, a most pleasing brookside walk.

Lum Mill is thought to be the oldest mill on Cowley Brook, though there is little trace on the ground today. Old records show that Adam de Hoghton and Thomas Banastre in 1396 gave John de Ravensargh the water mill at Le Lum on a yearly payment of 6s. 8d. Corn and oats were milled here well into the 1800s, clearly an ancient and important enterprise.

Four houses stand on the site now where once eighteen cottages of 'Lum Fooak' nestled. The mill was gutted by fire in 1825 and was a great loss to the local community.

Adjoining the mill site is an old stone quarry and the old smithy that still stands.

White Carr to Knowle Green

Cross brook by footbridge to take the pathway on the right upstream, over footbridge to follow lane up to old barn on corner. Go up the path to the right of the barn and follow pathway up, over footbridge and up the steps by the old mill to farm lane. Turn left and walk up to Knowle Green.

Knowle Green

The line drawing pictures the Manor House at Knowle Green. A dwelling has stood on this site since the early 14th century and at that time it was known as Dilworth Hall, later to be known as Cottam Hall, then Knoll Hall in the 19th century. The house has no datestone but given the architectural details it can be ascribed to the mid 17th century.

The Cottams were a notable family in the area and for many years resided at the Hall. Their most recounted member was one Father Thomas Cottam. a martyr to the Catholic faith. Thomas came from a Protestant family but received a liberal education; this led him to join the Jesuit Order in France. He was ordained at Rheims in 1580, then to be sent on the English mission.

He was arrested at Dover and sent before the Protestant ministers who brutally tortured him at Marshalsea in an effort to try to convert him. This failed and he was removed to the Tower to be racked and undergo the torture of the 'Scavenger's Daughter'.

After a year's confinement he was arraigned to Westminster Hall with Edmund Campion and others and condemned to death on the 14th November 1581. On the 13th May 1583, he was dragged on a hurdle from Newgate to Tyburn and was there hanged, drawn and quartered.

Knowle Green to Higher Birks

Opposite the church you will find a footpath sign. Walk along the track then enter rear of cottages on right to cross the lawn and pass over stile. Walk down to pass over footbridge and on up to pass through kissing gate. Follow stream up to enter Hoardsell farmyard and pass directly through and up to go through top field gate. Walk up the hill to the post and on to pass over wall-stile onto road. Pass through gate over on the left and walk along the wall to cross stream and on up the field in the direction of the mast to pass over wall-stile.

Continue on up to pass through gateway on left of sheds. Pass through the farmyard onto the roadway to enter the golf course via double gates. Walk directly on and down over the links to pass over fence-stile and on to enter wood via stiles. The path now leads down to Dale House via stiles. Walk on to go left between lower farm buildings to pass over stile. Cross the field to enter wood at stile and follow path on to pass over fence-stile. Walk along the edge of the wood to pass over next stile and on to cross footbridge. Walk on to enter Bradleys farmyard via gate. Leave by stile at gate and cross the field to enter White Fold farmyard via gate. Pass over wall-stile and follow hedgeline on to pass over stile and stream. Cross the field directly, over fence-stile and on to the roadway at Higher Birks via small gate.

Higher Birks

The farmer at Higher Birks informs me that the farmhouse was once an inn, known as 'The Dog and Pheasant'. The house dates back to 1663, and an inventory of the house's contents then does include more household goods and equipment than would be found in the average house of this type in those times. An inn, offering food and shelter, would account for this excess.

The front of the house is very grand, looking out over the Bowland Fells. It is Georgian and symmetrical in design, only at the rear can one see signs of the earlier building.

The low mullioned windows are wholly original, but the tall stair-well window is a composite of re-used mullions. On the roadside, near the rear, stands an old horse mounting block, again suggesting its former status as an inn.

At the bottom of the front garden, built into the wall, is an old lime kiln. Before firing the limestone the front would be bricked up. A close inspection will reveal traces of fired lime upon all the stonework and the remains of the back flu.

In the garden to the west of the house can be found the paved stones of a Donkey Walk — a shaft ran from this into the building on the end of the house that turned the stones to grind grain into flour. The grindstones are still in existence, stored in one of the buildings adjoining the house. What with fine ales, flour and bags of lime, the original owner must have been quite an entrepreneur!

The barn belonging to Higher Birks retains a single cruck 'A' frame mounted upon large stones. It is one of the few cruck built structures in the district.

Higher Birks to Written Stone

Walk up the road to leave by footpath signed on the left opposite a farm. Follow right-hand wall, over stiles, to road. Cross over stile opposite and walk straight on, over wall stile, to field gate. Cross road and follow track opposite to farm. Pass through farmyard, down the track and through the gate. Walk down the field on a slight left diagonal to corner clump of trees. Enter lane by gate and follow down to Written Stone Farm. The stone is set in the banking at the entrance to the farm.

The Written Stone

Inscribed upon the stone is the following text:

RAVFFE REDCLIFFE LAID THIS STONE TO LYE FOR EVER.
A.D. 1655.

Many fanciful stories have been woven around this stone, but none come
near to its true purpose. The stone was laid by Ralph Radcliffe at a time when
plague and other ills were reaping through Lancashire — if his and other seed
were lost to the future then at least the stone would testify to their existence.
Consider the following extract from a survey of Lancashire at the time (1646-
1650):

"In this County hath the plague of pestilence been raging for these three
years and upwards, occasioned chiefly by the wars. There is very great
scarcity and dearth of all provisions, especially of all sorts of grain, which is
fully six-fold the price that of late it has been.

"All trade, by which they have been much supported, is utterly decayed; it
would melt any good heart to see the numerous swarms of begging poor,
and the families that pine away at home, not having faces to beg. Very many
more now craving almes at other mens dores, who were used to give others
alms at their dores — to see the paleness, nay, death, appear in the cheeks of
the poor, and often to hear of some found dead in their houses, or on
highways, for want of bread".

Lancashire remained in an unsettled state until after the Rebellion of 1745,
after which the county grew and flourished in both trade and learning.

Written Stone to Buckley Gate

Follow farm lane down, over crossroads, down to the Cross Keys Hotel.

Walk 5

WHALLEY VILLAGE TRAIL

LUNCH: *The Swan Hotel*

It is possible to spend more than a full week in and around the village of Whalley and still not view fully its many varied sites and places of interest. So here I will restrict myself to only describing that which must be seen in order to appreciate the village's historical development and place in history.

Most people visit the Abbey and Parish Church, each having very good guide books on sale that I suggest you purchase and make good use of as I do not intend to repeat their contents here.

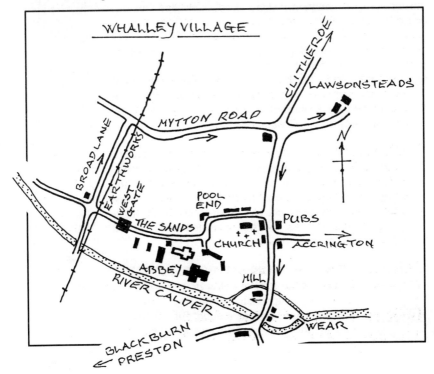

After parking your car make your way to the south porch of the parish church of St. Mary and All Saints. The church is usually open to the public from 10 a.m. to 4 p.m. with a break for lunch. Before going inside the edifice, we shall first look at the three standing crosses and the external fabric of the building.

The Three Churchyard Crosses

a) THE WESTERNMOST CROSS.

Originally panelled crosses of this type were carved of oak and brightly painted in red, yellow, green, blue and white. What we see here is an early 11th century stone copy of an earlier wooden one. Again, the stone cross would have been painted with the Norse/Celtic colours.

This Hiberno-Norse cross (so named after the second and third generation Irish Norwegians who settled in Lancashire in the 10th century whose artistic culture became dominant) is much worn, having once done service as a farm gate-post during the Commonwealth, there is now only one face discernable.

The central panel depicts a haloed saint with hands upraised in the ancient attitude of prayer between two serpents, possibly St. Michael. The panel immediately above shows the Pelican in her piety, and the one below contains the Dog of Berser, the Scandinavian emblem of eternity representing the Creator.

The other three panels are filled with beautiful interlacing geometrical patterns. Given certain light, a figure can also be made out on the side of the cross shaft. The mutilated cross-head belongs not to this shaft but to the easternmost cross, the original is now in Blackburn Museum.

b) THE CROSS OPPOSITE THE PORCH

This is in a fair state of preservation, although a portion of the upper shaft is missing. Originally it would have stood at around 10ft in height. All four sides are decorated with S-shaped scroll

and zig-zag pattern, the central theme being a figurative
vinescroll.

The arms of the cross-head are missing, the decorated
central boss remains with the lower moulded arm. The cross-base
contains zig-zag work around its upper surface. This cross can be
no later than the early 11th century but I strongly suspect that it
is much, much earlier.

c) THE EASTERNMOST CROSS

The cross-head is not original but carved in a late 14th century
Gothic style. The shaft is Hiberno-Norse of the early 11th century and is much worn yet, in evening light, scrollwork and two
haloed figures side by side can be made out. The panels are edged
with a pelleted border.

A fragment of this cross is built into the fabric of the chancel wall opposite,
below the second window from the east. Pelleting and traces of interlace can
clearly be made out.

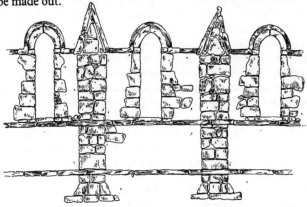

NORTH CHANCEL WALL, WHALLEY

The Church

We move on now to view the exterior of the building, starting with the chancel. For the most this belongs to the early 13th century, the north wall being
the best complete example and reminiscent of former Anglo-Saxon structures.

The chancel door (or Priest's Door) is also of this early period and still
retains the original ironwork and bronze head of the knocker. To the left
of this doorway, behind the cotoneaster, can be found two mediaeval grave

markers inscribed with crosses and a dagger, the only
ones that I know of in this part of Lancashire. Above
the running-window moulding on this south wall can
be found a decorated carved stone bearing the initials
I.H.S., its providence is unknown.

Passing the Late Perpendicular aisle and clerestory,
we move on to the mid-15th century tower that houses
eight bells (six plus a treble and tenor).

During the digging-out for the foundations for the
tower in c.1440, the workmen came across huge blocks
of masonry at a depth of four feet, some of which bore
figures and inscriptions from the Roman period. The Roman 'floor' provided
a good base on which the tower could be built, and fortunately a number of the
carved stones were kept to one side:

One, a large stone block containing a lewis hole and displaying herringbone
tooling, stands at the foot of the tower; another, to be found at the west end of
the north aisle, is an altar with a deity carved upon it in high relief said to be
Mars. This altar bears no inscriptions.

Built into the inner arch of the north door nearby is an inscribed stone
*FLAVIUS*VOT*OMPOSU (Flavius after fulfilment of his vow set this up).
Given the type of inscription one could put this work at c.270; a final stone is
now built into a wall at Standen Hall, being a relief of a standard-bearer.

Gravediggers, over the years, have found many Roman coins in the churchyard with recorded dates belonging to the 1st, 3rd
and 4th centuries A.D.

It can be ruled out that these stones and huge
blocks of masonry were brought from Ribchester
with good stone being available from Whalley Nab,
what we are stood upon is a very large Roman civil
settlement of which we shall hear more when looking at the Abbey grounds.

Upon entering the church, notice the many-scal-
loped capitals flanking the south doorway, the only
evidence of the Norman church that is mentioned in

THE PRIEST'S DOOR

Domesday when a Norman clerk recorded of Whalley that "Saint Mary's Church had two carucates of land exempt from all customary dues".

In the 10th century Whalley was the capital manor of a vast area of land that would be later known as Blackburnshire. This hundred was based on a Celtic pattern of land organisation — discrete estates divided into two commotes with its civil and ecclesiastical centre at the middle boundary of its two component parts.

Now that you are inside the church, you can purchase a guide book and gain insight to its many treasures; I shall go on to mention a few gems that the guide does not.

Firstly, when in the chancel, look behind the backrests of the Sedilia to find a large carved fragment of a pre-Conquest cross-shaft built into the stonework. Another fragment can be found in the wall behind the Bishop's throne (last seat nearest altar on the south choir stalls).

Above the north aisle, Mitton Chapel, altar (usually covered by a curtain) is mounted the Catholic pre-Reformation altar tablet with its five crosses — the wounds of Christ.

Behind the organ keyboard can be found panelwork displaying Jacobean workmanship. This, along with other pieces now housed in the tower, formed the pulpit in that time before the Commonwealth.

The small font by the side of the Roman altar came from the private chapel of John Paslew, last abbot of Whalley, at Wiswell Hall.

The Square and Church Lane

We now leave the churchyard by the west gate and proceed into the Square, the true centre of the old village. Before us face the three Jacobean cottages collectively known as Pool End, after a monastic fish-pond that stood to the north.

To the right is Church Lane, probably the oldest street in the village, containing a collection of cottages reflecting many periods of architecture. The one with the name 'The Blue Bell' used to be a village inn.

The village well, now covered by the road surface, once stood in the centre of the Square along with the village cross.

Whalley Abbey

We now walk down to enter the Abbey grounds by the castellated north gate. Pay the small admission fee and again purchase a guide book, read the Convent's full history later, for now content yourself with following the Abbey's layout plan. A scale model of the original convent layout can be found in the Gift Shop behind the ticket office — a must to see both before and after viewing the remains.

The Abbey dates from the early 14th century, built by the Cistercian monks of Stanlaw in the Wirral whose convent was being flooded and eroded by the tides and River Mersey. After the Dissolution, the Abbey and its lands were bought by John Braddyll and Richard Assheton, the latter taking the monastic site and buildings which he converted into a private house, now the Conference House for the Diocese of Blackburn. The initials of Richard Assheton, with a date 1588, are carved upon a stone that forms part of a buttress on the east wall of the house.

Recently, the Cumbria and Lancashire Archaeological Unit, housed at Lancaster University, have shown a great interest in the Abbey and surrounding area having carried out several surveys and some excavation work over the last four years. The foundations of the Abbey Corn Mill have been exposed and traced by a resistivity survey (see WHALLEY EARTHWORKS plan).

A drainage system, three feet below the Abbey drainage system, made up of well-cut arched stonework has been found to the south of the kitchen/refectory range. The evidence points to a Roman origin. Below the cobbled courtyard of the Conference House, at a depth greater than three feet, has been found another cobbled surface, but no providence can be put on it — could this be a Roman street?

The Chapel of Peter de Cestra

To the rear of the east wing of the Conference House are the remains of a small chapel associated with Peter of Chester, the first and only rector of Whalley. Prior to this office, Whalley Church was under the jurisdiction of Deans from Anglo-Celtic times until 1235. They were lords of the manor of Whalley, inheriting their positions from father to son.

The earliest recorded Dean was Spartling, followed by Liwulf, Cutwulf. Deans in Norman times were Henry, Robert, Henry, William, Galfridus, Geoffrey and Roger. The last Dean, complying with the Lateran Council of

1215, which forbade hereditary succession, gave up his ecclesiastical rights to John de Lacy, Earl of Lincoln, who appointed his clerk, Peter of Chester, to be rector.

The building is thought to be the private chapel of his rectory. The east window is divided into two simple lancets. In the south wall is a piscina with trifoliate bowl and there is an aumbry in the north wall. Later, the monks built their infirmary chapel over it.

Pope Nicholas IV gave the monks of Stanlaw permission to move to Whalley and take over the rectory on Peter's death. In 1296 they arrived and began to build their great Cistercian Abbey.

The Conference House Chapel

The House Chapel is situated on the ground floor and worth a visit if only to view two curious stones held there.

The first, known as the Brennand Stone, was brought here from Brennand House Farm and incorporated into the altar.

I consider the stone, marked IHS with five crosses, to be a portable altar stone. This type of stone could be carried in a saddle bag, thus enabling a lord to have the Mass said even when on hunting trips in the Forest of Bowland.

THE ANGEL STONE

The second stone stands by the window, this is the Slaidburn Angel Stone, a fragment of a Norse high cross. The stone depicts Volundr the Smith, with his artificial wings and holding his smithy tools.

His story can be found in the 'Lay of Volundr' in the collection of ancient Norse poems known as 'Verse Edda'. The small cross with knobbed ends is a swastica, the mark of Norse settlers. The coil or stopped plait is the Scandinavian Knot.

In truth, this stone really belongs in Slaidburn and I hope that one day it will be returned to that place.

THE SUN STONE

The Lay Brothers' Dormitory

Upon leaving the Abbey grounds and gardens by the North Gateway, we walk down The Sands to go left into the grounds of the Roman Catholic Church to view the Lay Brothers' Dormitory and Refectory, the most complete of the Convent buildings.

Lay-brothers lived by a rule less strict than that of the monks. Recruited from among the illiterate peasantry, they received no education, their main task being agricultural workers and running outlying granges (farms). When the Abbey became a private house this building was used as a barn for the newly built farmhouse (now the presbytery). It later served as a Catholic church and church hall.

Set at the north east corner of the building is a most curious gate post, known locally as the Whalley Abbey Sun Stone it has caused many to wonder as to its origins.

Contact with the local Catholic priest will prove rewarding for in his care are a number of objects of interest from the Abbey. The most important of these being the Sacred Relic of the Abbey — a fragment of the Swaddling Clothes of the new-born Infant Jesus held inside a leather bound hollow cross.

Another relic is the signet ring of John Paslew, last Abbot of Whalley. Other interesting items include a collection of decorated tiles from the floor of the Abbey Church, a statue of a headless monk holding a skull, numerous carved and decorated fragments of stonework, and a Celtic Head over two thousand years old. The latter was found when digging out for the gardens of the present church building.

Before leaving, wander into the church gardens to view the statue of Our Lady of Whalley. When the Abbey was first built this statue occupied an important niche in the main gate to the Abbey Church. After the Dissolution, it was cast ignominiously into the River Calder. It remained there for many centuries until it was discovered by some workmen; it was then placed on a pedestal in the church garden and a new devotion sprang up around it in the form of an annual May procession in which parishes from far and wide participate.

We now leave the Catholic Church to wander on down the road to view the West Gate of the Abbey.

The West Gate

The West Gateway is by far the most impressive of all the remains, being the oldest part of the Abbey buildings, having been erected in the early 14th century. Above the magnificent rib-vaulted ceiling is a large room with decorated windows all round. This was originally a chapel for the guests. The piscina and aumbry still remain. In later years it became a school-house from which the local Grammar School originated.

The small doorways at road level connected the Gate House to the Guest House or Hostelry, a two-storeyed building with nine bed chambers, and the Almonry where gifts of food and woollen cloth were given out to the poor.

Leaving the Gateway we now move on to view the Earthworks, after which we shall return to the village via Broad Lane and Mitton Road.

Journeys Through Brigantia

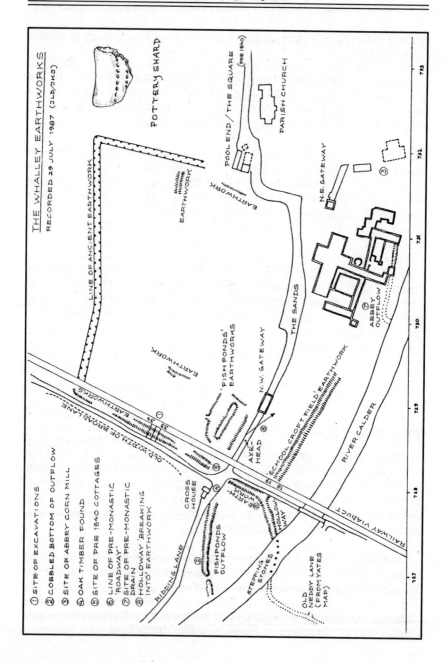

THE WHALLEY EARTHWORKS
RECORDED 29 JULY 1987 (OLD/3KO)

POTTERY SHARD

LINE OF ANCIENT EARTHWORK

EARTHWORK

EARTHWORK

POOL END / THE SQUARE

(PRE 1840)

PARISH CHURCH

N.E. GATEWAY

③

EARTHWORK

THE SANDS

ABBEY
OUTFLOW

⑦

N.W. GATEWAY

'FISHPONDS'
EARTHWORKS

AXE-
HEAD ⑥

SCHOOL CROFT FIELD EARTHWORK

RIVER CALDER

"OLD WIDTH OF BROAD LANE"
EARTHWORKS

35

①

⑤

CROSS
HOUSE

④

EARTH
WORK

⑧

HOLLOWAY
WAY

RAILWAY VIADUCT

RIDDING LANE

②
FISHPONDS
OUTFLOW

STEPPING
STONES

OLD
NEDDY LANE
(FROM YATES
MAP)

① SITE OF EXCAVATIONS
② COBBLED BOTTOM OF OUTFLOW
③ SITE OF ABBEY CORN MILL
④ OAK TIMBER FOUND
⑤ SITE OF PRE 1840 COTTAGES
⑥ LINE OF PRE-MONASTIC 'ROADWAY'
⑦ SITE OF PRE-MONASTIC DRAIN
⑧ HOLLOWAY 'BREAKING INTO' EARTHWORK

The Whalley Earthworks

Standing above the village of Whalley is the Iron Age hillfort of Portfield. Excavations on this redoubt suggest settlement as early as 2000 B.C. and use as a fortified position up to the 7th century A.D. What Portfield represented over the latter half of this time span was only a component part of a larger settlement being the high retreat in troubled times.

By 1250 B.C. man had come down from his high homesteads on the surrounding hills and begun the clearance of the valley floor for settlement and cultivation. One dominant group colonized that rich area between Langho and Worston siting Whalley as their administrative centre, a geographical choice displaying a high degree of forward planning in the formation of a structured society — a far cry from the incrementalism displayed by today's leaders and planners.

When the first dwelling was erected at Whalley we do not know, in fact only the chance find of a stone axe-hammer testify to man's presence on the site (now in Preston Museum). The surmise can only be based on a later continuity of settlement and Whalley's importance during major events in pre-Conquest history.

First mention of Whalley can be found in Bede and the Anglo-Saxon Chronicle for the year 664. During that year Bishop Tuda visited these areas west of the Pennines to oversee the submission of the Celtic Church to Roman rites. While in Whalley, he died of the outbreak of bubonic plague recorded for that year, an horrific slayer that was given its momentum by the Synod of Whitby. Bede goes on to state that Whalley (Paegnalaech) was the site of a monastery. Clearly this was an important religious settlement, fit for a bishop to base himself on, on a pastoral visit.

All that remains today of that early religious institution is the 'vallum monasterii', an earthen banked ditch. This latter served as a spiritual and legal boundary for the convent and must not be regarded as defensive, although in a previous age it may well have been first constructed for this purpose.

Between 1985 and 1988 an archaeological investigation conducted by myself and the Department of Geophysics at Lancaster University on the earthworks has revealed its true site plan and method of construction. Fragments of 7th century pottery along with other artefacts were found during the excavations at a depth of 3ft in the bottom section of the ditch. Work will continue and should prove most rewarding, casting light on the village's ancient past.

Whalley is again mentioned in the Anglo-Saxon Chronicle for the year 798 as the site of a decisive battle in an internal conflict that had fraught the kingdom of Northumbria for over twenty years. Then a hundred and fifty years later three high crosses are erected at Whalley; each event a reflection of the local importance of Whalley between the 8th and 10th centuries.

The presence of an early monastic institution may go some way to explain the office of hereditary Deans at Whalley Church before the advent of Peter of Chester in 1235. Whalley, in pre-Norman times, was the caput (capital) of the cantrev (hundred) of Blackburnshire (possibly a former name existed).

The cantrev was divided into two commotes (component parts) represented by the mediaeval parishes of Whalley and Blackburn. Each commote contained two royal vills — Pendleton and Huncoat, Walton-le-Dale and Blackburn respectively, all dependent on the royal caput at Whalley (other vills existed but only these royal ones are recorded in the Norman Survey). Whalley would be the site of not only the court of the local petty dynasty but of a minster.

Founded by a nobleman on his estate, ruled by his relatives and staffed by his dependants, it would be a 'family monastery' with most of the functions of a parish church. The founding of these royal minsters under royal licence was a way of diverting taxable resources due to the King (of Northumbria) back to one's own family by grants of land, labour and capital to the 'church' (tax evasion on a grand scale was as commonplace then as it is now).

It was the disintegration of the royal resource base in this way that led to the downfall of Northumbria to the Scandinavians. The society could no longer mobilise in its own defence under various Kings heading only factions of a greater political whole.

The hereditary principle established within the framework of the family 'minster/church' seems to have been held in practice at Whalley, possibly due to its Northumbrian 'remoteness', until the 13th century — remarkable! Is there a foundation for the 'Statutes of Blackburnshire' after all?

The Return Leg via Lawsonsteads/Manor House

A wander up Broad Lane following the railway arches brings us on to Mitton Road. Turn right and walk on to the junction with the main road at Stocks Hill, named after the old siting of the village stocks. Here stands the former Whalley Grammar School. The present building dates from 1725 and the original Charter for the school was issued in 1549 and founded from the former school in the chapel of the old West Gate of the Abbey.

We cross the road now to walk up Brooks Lane opposite. At the far end of the lane stands Lawsonsteads and the building known as the Manor House. Once the home of the Brooks family, Lancashire bankers and developers, Whalley Range in Manchester was built by one of the family. The house dates from the late 16th century and inside can be found a massive inglenook fireplace with a beehive bread oven.

Built into the barn at Lawsonsteads are a number of decorated fragments of stonework from the Abbey, and across the way is an open-air museum of bygone farm machinery and implements, all delightfully placed and maintained.

Make your way back now to the centre of the village. At the old Town Gate, marked by the new mini-roundabout, stand the four Whalley inns; the Dog, the Swan, the De Lacy and the Whalley Arms, serving well the inhabitants of the village who sway leisurely between these watering holes. The De Lacy Arms is built on the site of the ancient Manor House of Whalley and a well from that former place still exists under the saloon bar floor. At the rear of the pub once stood the old charnel house, now an insignificant small building housing garden implements.

We make our way now in the direction of Whalley Bridge. Down an alley on the right can be found the Whalley Corn Mill complete with timber water-wheel that powered the enterprise till 1961. The millrace, which once turned the wheel of the monks' corn mill in the Abbey grounds, can be followed along its length back to the impressive wear, also built by the monks.

And now back to Whalley Bridge to gaze awhile up river at the tumbling waters of this rapid provider of former power.

Walking back into the village, notice Bridge Cottage on the right. It was here that Harrison Ainsworth stayed when researching his novel "The Lancashire Witches". Further on we come to an old Tudor farmstead now known as the Toby Jug. The house is of cruck construction and contains much original oak panelling, all carefully preserved by the owners.

Well that is the end of our little trail. Hopefully it has been a rewarding one, giving you some insight into the village's ancient past and connections.

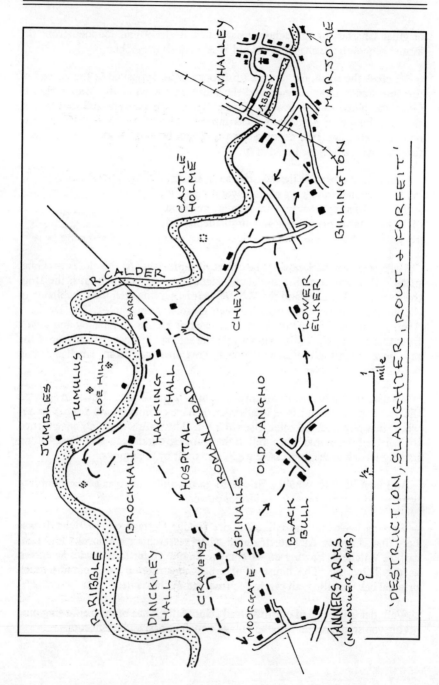

3/12/93

Walk 6

DESTRUCTION, SLAUGHTER, ROUT AND FORFEIT

Whalley, Billington, Hacking, Brockhall,
Dinckley and Old Langho

8 Miles, 4 hours

MAP: *O.S. sheet SD 63/73 PATHFINDER*

LUNCH: *Black Bull, Old Langho*

START: *Whalley Village*

Since being a young boy the village of Whalley and the meeting of the rivers has always held a fascination for me, for here is a place of battle, crumbling ruins and burial mounds — all grist to child's imagination.

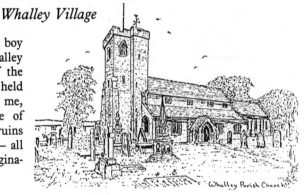

Whalley Parish Church

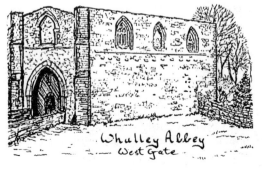

Whalley Abbey West Gate

The walk described here is my favourite walk in the Ribble Valley bringing back many fond memories. Before I describe the walk I include an essay by my brother, Phillip, on the 1643 battle of Whalley, an event often mentioned but rarely examined.

THE BATTLE OF WHALLEY 1643
Context & Consequences

The Civil War in Lancashire 1642 to 1644 was a regional struggle related to, but separate from the National conflict. This essay will examine the events which led to the engagement at Whalley in April 1643 and the consequences of the Parliamentary victory.

THE CIVIL WAR IN LANCASHIRE
September 1642 - April 1643

SEPTEMBER 1642. Revolutionary events in London and Westminster divide the Nation. All over England and Wales supporters of the King and Parliamentary factions attempt to seize local magazines (stores of arms and powder etc). By July 1642 all magazines in Lancashire had been seized for the King — with the exception of Manchester, the key Parliamentary stronghold in the county. Most of the county stood for the King — support for the Parliament was only to be found in certain textile towns in Blackburnshire and Salford Hundreds. In September 1642 Lord Strange (later Lord Derby) tried to seize Manchester, but his siege of the town was fruitless. At the end of the month Manchester, Bolton and Blackburn stood for the Parliament.

OCTOBER 1642. The Manchester garrison take Bury, Rochdale and the only Royalist outpost in the east of Blackburnshire, Towneley Hall, Burnley.

NOVEMBER 1642. Sir Gilbert Hoghton briefly takes Blackburn and disarms Parliamentary supporters in Whalley, but is defeated and routed by Col. Shuttleworth and Col. Starkie in a night attack to retake Blackburn. Royalist victory in a skirmish at Westhoughton.

DECEMBER 1642. Hoghton again tries to take Blackburn (24th December) for the King, but fails.

JANUARY 1643. Skirmish at Salesbury Hall, little fighting due to season of the year.

FEBRUARY 1643. Troops from the Parliamentary towns of Manchester, Bolton and Blackburn storm Preston. Many leaders of the King's cause in Blackburnshire captured (February 8th). Royalist forces counter by attacking Bolton but were driven off. Troops from the Parliamentary garrison at Preston take Lancaster (end of February).

MARCH 1643. On March 13th Lord Derby left Wigan with 600 foot and 400 horse, he crossed the Ribble at Freckleton and by March 18th had taken Lancaster town, but the Castle garrison held out against him. A relief force moved north from Preston, while Derby moved south. The two forces passed each other (a couple of miles apart) about seven miles south of Lancaster. Lancaster was retaken for the Parliament, but Derby coming on to Preston found the town nearly devoid of troops, and so retook the town for the King. This success was followed up by an assault on Bolton, which was beaten-off with 25 of the King's men lying dead around the town.

The next blow came on Easter eve when the Manchester and Bolton garrisons stormed Wigan. Though the town was sacked, no attempt was made to take Warrington for Parliament. The plan was for Parliamentary forces from Cheshire to assist the Manchester garrison, but with little help from Cheshire in this respect. Lord Derby took command in the town and the Manchester garrison was unable to enter the town. Derby having successfully held Warrington removed to Preston.

On the eve of the Battle of Whalley, Warrington, Preston, Wigan and Liverpool were held for the King. Bolton, Bury, Blackburn, Rochdale and Manchester and its environs stood for Parliament. There was also an insulated Parliamentary garrison at Lancaster. Clearly the county was divided fairly finely with Salford and Blackburn hundreds for the Parliament, and the rest of the county for the King. At Preston in the second week of April 1643 a general muster of Royalist forces raised a force of 11 troops of horse, 700 foot and several thousand 'clubmen' from the Fylde. Within 48 hours of the main Royalist field army in Lancashire leaving Preston it had ceased to exist as a military unit — the King's cause in Lancashire was in ruins.

THE BATTLE OF WHALLEY
April 20th 1643

Lord Derby left Preston at dawn on April 19th 1643, a Wednesday. Keeping north of the Ribble they must have reached Ribchester well before noon, and Whalley by later in the afternoon. The only Parliamentary troops nearby fell back from the Dunkenhalgh Hall at Clayton-le-Moors to Padiham where Parliamentary forces rallied at Gawthorpe, the home of Colonel Shuttleworth. Local forces rallied at Gawthorpe on the morning of the 20th, but Shuttieworth had only 500 local foot and 5 troops of horse.

Derby slept at Whalley Abbey on the night of the 19th. Broxup* believes that he waited at Whalley expecting the local Parliamentary forces to attack. For whatever reason the fact is that Derby waited at Whalley for nearly 24 hours and in so doing lost the initiative.

Sometime towards noon the vanguard of Derby's force left Whalley on the road towards Padiham. The road to Padiham as we know it now did then not exist. The route to Great Harwood was via the Calder Bridge at Whalley and up the Nab via Whalley Banks and onwards to Cliffe and from here to Great Harwood. The route to Padiham left Whalley between the Swan and the Whalley Arms (these public houses did not exist at this period). The track went up the hill to Portfield Bar, on down to Read Old Bridge and on over the Heights to Padiham.

It was along the road to Read that the battle began. The vanguard of Derby's forces under Colonel Tyldesley advanced around the middle of the day, passed Portfield Farm and down into the dell of Sabden Brook. Let us now consider the problems facing Colonel Shuttleworth and his Parliamentary forces.

Colonel Shuttleworth decided on the morning of the 20th to fall back on Padiham and Burnley rather than face such a superior force. However, the rank and file took matters into their own hands. On being told to fall back they told their officers:

"Being resolute men replied to their captains boldly bidding them take what course pleased for their own safety, yet they would adventure themselves, see the enemy and have one bout with them, if God will."

Shuttleworth, faced with such resolve, set an ambush above the Sabden Brook. We can assume that the ale houses of Whalley had been drunk dry and there may well have been many thick heads that morning. Troops raised on the coast of the Fylde and West Derby may not have been used to moving in hill country, so increasing the tension. There was clearly no warning as the Royalist troops marched out of the dell. On a dry April morning 500 firearms rang out, blood and death was to fill the morning air.

The Royalist forces, being strung out along the narrow lane, could only fall back, first on Portfield and then on Whalley. Derby made no attempt to stand and fight, his fate was sealed. A body of men which starts to run in disarray ceases to be an army. Troops at ease in Whalley saw the remains of the vanguard fleeing, cut about and hard pressed. Terror spread in the Royalist ranks, they could not know that they had an advantage in arms of three to one. For all they knew, this could have been the vanguard of the Manchester Parliamentary field army pressing down on them. The Royalist forces in Whalley were not in a state of defence, men began to slip away, arms cast aside.

Within a very short time the whole of the Royalist army was in flight across the Calder towards Ribchester. Only the main part of the horse under Derby escaped as a military unit. Shuttleworth pursued the routed troops as far as Salesbury ferry. Derby fled beyond Preston to Penwortham Hall before he slept that night. Within a fortnight he had left for the Isle of Man, the King's cause being all but lost in Lancashire.

With the defeat of the Royalists at Whalley, the forces of the Parliament quickly moved to take Wigan (April 22nd). The remains of the Royalist horse under Colonel Tyldesley and Molneux were driven northwards out of the county. These forces joined up with the Royalist forces in Yorkshire. Preston, devoid of its garrison, was taken. Liverpool's Royalist garrison also fled at this time. Warrington was besieged in mid May and fell on the 28th of that month due to lack of provisions.

Hornby and Thurland Castles fell in June 1643, leaving only Latham House (Wigan) and Greenhalgh Castle (Garstang) for the King in Lancashire. So by June Lancashire was firmly in the hands of Parliament, as it was to remain — except for the brief interlude of bloody Prince Rupert in the summer of 1644 — for the rest of the Civil War.

Two questions arise from the Battle of Whalley:

1. Why was the Royalist field army so utterly routed?

2. What was Derby's reason to march on Whalley from Preston?

Clearly Derby should have pressed on instead of letting his men stand down at Whalley, but basically we have poor quality troops and foolish officers, this was the cause of the rout. The ambush in the Sabden Brook dell points to no scouting and the large body of Royalist troops in Whalley should have been put on a defensive footing. The story of the rout points to a lack of good order and discipline, the basic foundation of any military unit. The Parliamentary forces executed a fine ambush and pressed home their advantage. It is clear that the rank and file believed in what they were fighting for; these men were right to defend their homes and also had the advantage of the local terrain.

We are now left with the question: why did Derby strike out from Preston into Blackburnshire — via an odd route. If he wished to secure Preston, why did he not march directly against the modest defences of Blackburn town? Was his plan to suprise the heartland of Protestant Blackburnshire by a blow against the Calder Valley? If so why did he wait at Whalley? Maybe he wanted to secure communications and supplies with Royalist forces in north Yorkshire. If this was his aim why then did he not garrison Clitheroe — and therefore hold the road to Skipton and York.

It has been put to me by J. L. Dixon that Derby having taken Preston by a suprise march, may have been aiming to march on Manchester via Burnley, Rochdale and Bury. The advantage of this plan was that Derby would have been able to pick up support in Rochdale and Bury and come against Manchester from an unexpected direction.

For myself, I draw no conclusion whatsoever. The long-term plan, the march on Whalley, was poorly executed once Derby's field army stood down in the village. The advance from Whalley was logical, but too long delayed. I conclude that the main cause of the rout was Lord Derby himself.

* *"The Civil War in Lancashire"* *Ernist Broxup. Man. Univ. 1910.*

Whalley Village to Chew Mill

Make your way down Church Street and into The Sands to pass through the west gateway of Whalley Abbey. Turn left at the junction and cross the Calder to follow the railed-off pathway to pass through the Sunnyside Avenue kissing gate. Walk on to pass over stile and follow path towards electricity sub-station to pass over stile and onwards to cross the by-pass (be careful, some treat this as a motorway. Really, the county council should put a footbridge or underpass in here). The footpath now follows the overhead cables to the roadway at Chew Mill via footbridge and stile.

Chew Mill

Chew Mill farm, the Old Mill Cottage and the 'Great Tree of Billangahoh' are all that remain of the ancient hamlet of Chew that existed here for many centuries. The manor house at Potter Ford has gone, the bobbin mill converted (the mill-race from the Calder remains) and the Judge Walmsley Inn has moved to above the bridge at Whalley.

Chew stood on an important route that connected Whalley with Blackburn and all points west. The medieval roads from Wilpshire and Ribchester are for the most part today only recognisable as crop-marks and raised bankings. In times past these met at Chew Mill ford to enter the village of Whalley by Riddings Lane. The western access to and from the Cistercian Convent also followed the Chew highway.

North-east from Chew, in a field by the Calder 'horseshoe', stands a square raised mound known as Castle Holme (permission to view must be obtained from the friendly farmer at Chew). The mound is 70ft. square and rises about 5ft. above the surrounding ground facing the cardinal points. The mound is thought to be the site of a Roman temple or station, given its size and close proximity to the civil settlement at Whalley. Roman coins of Hadrian were found on the site in the 1830s.

The position of this ancient structure is a good site for a post for securing the passage of the river Calder, as it is placed between two fords, Potterford and Chew Mill Ford. Over the first passed the Roman road from Ribchester to York, and the old road from Blackburn to Whalley passed over the second.

Chew Mill to Hacking Hall

Follow the road over Bushburn Bridge and up the hill to the lane opening on the right. Walk down the left-hand farm lane and follow it around to the right (this section is part of the Roman road) down to pass Hacking barn to the front of the Hall.

Hacking Hall

This magnificent Jacobean mansion stands at the confluence of the Calder and the Ribble. Recently restored it is resplendent with its many mullioned gabled frontage. The hall was built by Thomas Livesey, father of Sir Thomas Walmesley's mother, in 1607 and later added to by Judge Walmesley of Dunkenhalgh. The original timber-framed manor house stood on the moated site of Chete Yard, a position to the side of the present building.

The principal room of the first floor of the east wing was formerly panelled in richly carved oak, one compartment of which bore the arms of the Judge. The panelling was removed sometime before 1875 and taken to Dunkenhalgh.

The great barn at Hacking is an old tithe barn built by the convent at Whalley. The massive cruck-frame structure gives it a church-like appearance. Permission is needed to view the inside of the barn.

The place-name 'Hacking' refers to an apparatus with a net attached, used for taking fish from the river and gave name to a local family.

Across the Ribble can be seen the old boatman's house, Loe Hill, and the Bronze Age tumulus.

Hacking Hall to Dinckley Hall

Enter the field facing the hall front and walk on to the riverbank. Walk downriver to enter wood via stile. Make your way through the wood to leave by stile. Walk up to the left to follow trackway up to enter Brockhall farm yard. Pass through gate on right and cross the bank of the field to pass over stile. Walk down and past the former playing fields and market gardens to pass over a stile by a white gate. Follow hawthorn and privet lined path on to pass over footbridge (since the closure of the hospital the orchards here have fallen into decay, and is a sad sight to see. Sadder still is the sight of former patients wandering forlorn and neglected in the hostile streets of Burnley, Blackburn and Preston).

Walk up and pass over the stile and on around the old barn to enter field. Cross the field on a left diagonal to enter Craven Fold farm. After a few steps down the farm drive pass through the gap in the hedge on the right and walk on to pass through gate. Walk on to the wall-stile at Cravens (a very good example of modern building), but do not pass over the stile. Instead, walk down to the right to pass over stile by gate on left. Follow line of left-hand hedge on and down to pass over stile on left. Cross the field keeping the wood to your right to enter Dinckley Hall Lane via gate. The lane leads down to Dinckley Hall and permission must be sought to view the cruck-built gable of the house.

Dinckley Hall

Dinckley Hall, a two storey cruck-framed farmhouse, is little altered from its original central hall and projecting wings. The north wing has disappeared, and some parts have been rebuilt in brick. However, the east gable and the central hall retain their ancient timber cruck construction, pointing to a date of around 1450. Inside the house the massive cruck timbers dominate every angle, and with the great fireplace the interior is very imposing indeed.

The south wall has two large projecting stone chimneys, one carried on corbels. On the east side is part of an enclosing garden wall with a stone pier and ball at the angle, and from here one can see the picturesque timber gable.

Up to the 15th century the Cliderows resided here. They were followed by the Talbots, Lords of Salesbury and Bashall, great landowners in the Ribble Valley. The Hall's most notable occupant was John Talbot, who forfeited his estate to the Treason trustees for joining the King at Worcester in 1651, during the second Civil War.

In around 1610, a report on the clergy stated that at Dinckley there was a 'chapel but no reader'. Nothing is known of the chapel, though some suppose it to be the barn adjoining the Hall. I personally think it stood in the south-west corner of the Parish near the boundary stone below Wheatley Farm, Salesbury. The field name here is 'Chapel Field', and the field itself is too small to be of any agricultural use.

A number of Roman altars have been found in the grounds of the Hall, one of which was used as a cheese-press before 1725.

The place-name Dinckley is of Celtic origin and means 'fortified place in the wooded lea', Interestingly, the name of the neighbouring parish of Salesbury means 'fortified place among the willows'. The two may refer to one and the same place, being a once fortified British settlement of some note.

Dinckley Hall to Old Langho

Return up the lane to take the lane on the left, passing Moorgate Farm along the Roman road to Aspinalls (the buildings here are part of a once tannery complex. A conical-shaped edging stone and a Roman altar, rutted with wear, were found built into the old stables here. These are now on display in Ribchester Museum).

Pass directly through Aspinalls to go through far gate. Cross the field on a right diagonal towards a pair of oaks, then follow the path down into the valley to cross a footbridge. Walk up and to the right of the group of trees and on to the mock-Tudor Black Bull via gate. St. Leonard is off the road to the left.

St. Leonard, Old Langho

The church of St. Leonard is said to have been built in 1557, with stone from the dismantled Whalley Abbey.

Many of the stones are covered with ecclesiastical designs in the form of carvings. Inside the Stoup (Holy Water font) and Piscina (basin for washing the communion or mass vessels) may have come from the same source.

The bench ends are carved with the initials of their owners with dates from 1688 to 1692. Ancient fragments of glass can be seen in the south-east window. In summer the chapel is hidden by a profusion of leafage and provides a welcome shade from the hot sun.

Old Langho is the original village centre, the other villages of Langho and Billington only coming with the building of Whalley New Road. The earlier road ran from the New Inns, above Blackburn, along the top of Billington Moor then down to Whalley.

Elkar, at Billington, is the site of an ancient hamlet. On one of the old houses can be seen a carved corbel showing an angel holding a shield, this stone may also have come from Whalley Abbey.

The name Langho is a shortened version of the ancient spelling of Billington, Billangahoh. The name comes from a Folk known as the Billingas, a Brigantian tribe that occupied the land between Whalley Nab, Billinge above Blackburn and Hoghton Bottoms at the time of the Roman occupation.

Old Langho to Whalley

On leaving the church follow the road to the left to turn right at Keepers Cottage (B & B, licensed restaurant, dated 1725). Carry on along the road passing Hillock Farm (notice the stone bearing a lion rampant and the initials of Thomas Hoghton) and Skenning Bridge to pass through the field gate on the left. Cross the field towards Pendle to pass over stile and on to pass over next stile in far right corner. Walk on, across the stream and up to pass over stile. Follow path on, passing a lone oak to pass over stile near farm.

The old farm track leads past the rear of the barn where we pass over a stile and walk on to the farm drive. The drive leads us down to Elker Lane. We now walk up the lane to cross the new by-pass then enter the old section of Elker Lane on the left. Walk on to pass over a stile on the right and pass over footbridge. Walk on heading for the far black field gate and after passing through follow the hedge round to pass through Whittams farmyard. Follow the lane down to the left to Sunnyside Avenue and retrace your steps back to Whalley.

Terrace Row and Marjorie

Since being a young boy Terrace Row has always held a fascination for me. I used to imagine myself sitting on the balcony watching the skirmish between Roundhead and Cavalier on Whalley Bridge, such are a young boy's thoughts. The five early 19th century cottages, with their Gothic windows and access balcony, are a true delight to the eye.

The Marjorie, in the same Gothic style, stands on the bank of the river Calder just above Whalley Bridge. Walk up the river and you will notice a large weir. The mill-race leading from it connects it to an old corn mill, which even today is complete with its old wooden water-wheel.

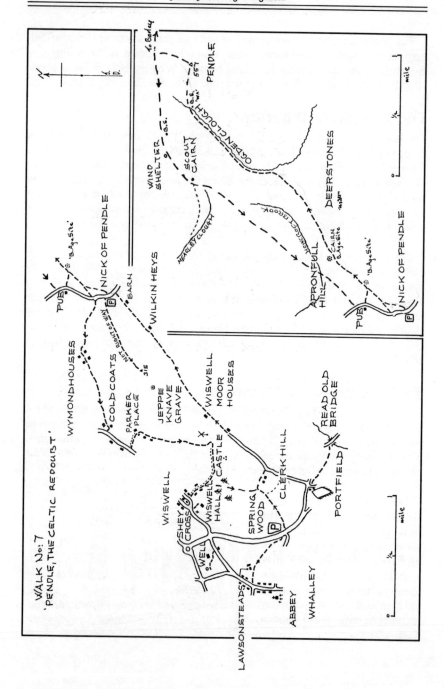

WALK No: 7
'PENDLE, THE CELTIC REDOUBT'

Walk 7

PENDLE, THE CELTIC REDOUBT

Spring Wood, Nick of Pendle, Pendle, Wymondhouses and Wiswell

13½ miles, 6 hours

MAP:	*O.S. sheets SD 63/73, 64/74, 84/94 PATHFINDER*
LUNCH:	*Well Springs, Nick of Pendle*
START:	*Spring Wood car park above Whalley (A.671)*

This walk takes us from above the Whalley gorge and along the spine of Pendle to the summit cairn. In the early days of our history this hill gave shelter and life to farmers and workers in stone and bronze, who later moved from their hilltop redoubt to clear and settle the valley floors.

Signs of that early time are to be seen in the number of mounds and ring-banked cairns scattered over the higher ground, Jeppe Knave Grave denuded tumulus and Devil's Apronfull ring-banked cairn to name but two.

Finds of man's early tools have been few; as is only to be expected, time and the build up of peat tend to put all things out of reach.

Spring Wood Car Park to Clerk Hill

Come out of the car park and walk to the left to pass over stile onto the golf course. Follow left-hand fence up to pass over footbridge on left. Walk up the field diagonally to follow fence up to go over stile and walk up to pass over two stiles. Follow the wall round the rear of Clerk Hill to the driveway. Walk along the driveway to the road (the grounds of Clerk Hill are private).

Clerk Hill

Clerk Hill

In the 13th century Clerk Hill was named Snelleshowe meaning 'the hill of Sniallr'. Sniallr or Snell would have been numbered among those Hiberno-Norse that erected the crosses in the churchyard at Whalley, if that place was their original siting.

The charming Georgian mansion that stands at Clerk Hill today was built by the Whalley family between 1715 and 1772. The site comes to note during a somewhat less charming period of our history: the earlier house that stood here was the home of the notorious John Hammond, renowned for his brutal torture of the Catholic priest Edmund Campion.

To the north-east of Clerk Hill stands Castle Wood, in which can be found the ruins of a once castellated folly known as Baby House Towers. Sadly this was demolished during the 1940s by men of the Royal Engineers under the instruction of a local farmer, annoyed by people visiting the site.

Down the road from Clerk Hill stands the hillfort of Portfield. Permission to view the earthworks must first be sought from the owners of Portfield House.

Portfield Hillfort

Portfield is the birthplace of my lifelong friend, John Mitchell, with whom I spent my youth exploring all things of an ancient nature. Incredibly, his home was the most ancient of all.

The farmhouse stands on the site of Portfield Hall, home of the Braddyll family whose original seat was the the House of Braddyll with Brockhall on the banks of the Ribble. When the Hall was demolished the stones were used to build the Whalley Arms Inn. An old window from the Hall can be seen in the gable of the Inn, and with it a date 1781 and the initials R.C.

PORTFIELD HALL

The Great Barn of Portfield was erected by the monks of Whalley Abbey as a tithe barn; a tithe was a tenth part of agricultural produce paid as a tax. The timber construction within is the finest surviving example of early 14th century workmanship in the entire area.

Until recent times, Portfield was thought to be the site of a Roman camp or signal station. However, the findings of the summer of 1966 during pipe-laying operations across the site, changed the thinking on the early history of Lancashire.

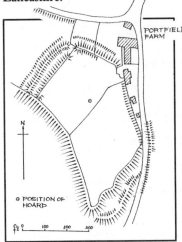

The camp lies on a slight southward-facing promontory. Clear traces of defensive works exist on the north-west. These consist of a bivallate bank and ditch structure. Further defences probably existed on the east and south-east, but no traces survive.

The 1960s excavation revealed two phases of construction. The earliest consisted of a single, stone-revetted rampart without a ditch situated some 20ft. behind the present inner rampart. The first rampart was subsequently levelled and the existing inner rampart constructed. This was again revetted in stone on its inner and outer faces having a clay core. It was separated from its ditch by a berm 20ft. wide. The outer bank and ditch may originally have had a slight counterscarp bank.

This early investigation redefined the camp as an Iron Age hill fort. The discovery of a Bronze Age hoard deposited in the 7th century B.C., revealed in the 1966 pipe laying operations, lends support to the idea that many of the hilltops later fortified in the Iron Age, as is the case at Portfield, may have originated as settlements even as early as 2000 B.C.

Portfield Camp is one of five hillforts, all in North Lancashire. With the exception of a large camp at Warton Crag the forts are all small in comparison with the great fortified earthworks of the South and reflect the broken nature of the countryside and a smaller more scattered population. The siting of the hoard near the junction of the river Calder with the Ribble points to a still active trade link along a trans-Pennine route of long standing.

The Portfield Hoard

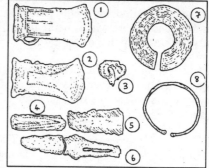

1. Bronze, single-looped, socketed axe, sub-rectangular at mouth, with quadrangular body and expanded curved cutting-edge. Heavy moulding at the mouth with lighter moulding beneath from which descend three vertical, parallel ribs. Two vertical mouldings inside the socket.

2. Bronze, single-looped, socketed axe, oval at mouth, with octagonal faceted body and expanded curved cutting edge. Deep but slight moulding at the mouth.

3. Piece of rough bronze resembling a splash with bent-over runner.

4. Lower half of a bronze socketed gouge, lacking mouth and cutting-edge.

5. Part of a bronze blade with broad central thickening and bevelled edge.

6. Two pieces forming a tanged knife with central rib on each side of tang. The lower part of the blade is missing and much of the bronze cutting edges are corroded.

7. Gold penannular tress-ring of hollow triangular section, decorated with fine concentric incised lines made with a tracer. The ring is an Irish import and shows the maintenance of Hibernian contact at this period.

8. Gold plain penannular bracelet of flattened, slightly hollow D-section with externally expanded terminals. This is a 7th century B.C. copy in gold of the variant type of Covesea bronze bracelet. The gold is Irish but this type of bracelet is unknown in Ireland and therefore must have been made in or for the British northern market.

A flint arrowhead was found on the site in 1974, and is dated c.750 B.C.

Replicas of the hoard can be seen in both Ribchester and Blackburn Museums. The small fragment of rough metal (No. 3), clearly a by-product of smelting, shows that the hoard was the property of an actual bronze-smith. Recent excavations on the site have produced finds of Mesolithic flints, Neolithic Grimston ware and Beaker pottery as well as Late Bronze Age/Early Iron Age and Romano/British finds all pointing to the importance of the hill at Portfield through prehistoric times.

Clerk Hill to Nick of Pendle

Follow the road up to Wiswell Moor Houses, then follow the well-defined trackway to pass the rear of Wilkin Heys and on passing Parsley Barn to the Sabden Road. Walk up to the Nick.

A path leads south-west along the ridge to the Trig. Pt. summit of Wiswell Moor. Beyond this the land falls and in a hollow there are the group of stones known as 'Jeppe Knave Grave'. The site belongs to Parker Place Farm and permission is required to visit the site.

Jeppe Knave Grave

To the west of Wilkin Heys, just below the triangulation point, is a small depression in the moorland turf containing rocks and stones of various sizes. Upon the largest stone are inscribed the words 'JEPPE KNAVE GRAVE' and a cross. The stone is said to mark the final resting place of Jeppe Curteys, a local robber who was decapitated for his crimes in the first year of Edward III, 1327.

In those times the punishment of decapitation was unusual, being reserved for those of noble birth. The full story of Jeppe's crimes and trial would no doubt make an intriguing one indeed.

The grave spot itself is now thought to mark the site of a Bronze Age denuded tumulus, being a circular feature of around 20ft. in diameter. The outer ring of stones can be discerned in the rough pasture at the perimeter — yellow in dry conditions, showing the circular shape.

A mile north-west of the site is Carriers Croft where in 1968 another circular feature was discovered. During the excavation between 1968 and 1975, three collared urns along with a gold cylinder and a bone toddle were found. These are now on display in Clitheroe Castle Museum.

The Devil's Apronfull

This ring of stones stands upon the highest point of Pendleton Moor by the pathway that leads from the Nick of Pendle to the summit. The site is now recognised as a Bronze Age ring bank cairn, a paved outer ring with a central cairn of loose stones. Due to natural erosion and the absence of the build-up of peat, this feature can clearly be discerned at ground level, all that remains of a once communal living hut over 3,000 years old. The outer ring is all that remains of the stone outer wall, the inner cairn the central hearth, all roofed by timbers covered in turf in much the same way as the old Highland crofts.

Urn burials beneath the floor level are very common in these structures, only an excavation would establish the case here. A worthwhile task for some local archaeology group.

The Nick to Pendle Summit

A broad track leaves the road near to the car park and leads us on past Apronfull Hill up and over Black Hill into the upper reaches of Ogden Clough. We now follow the clough up to meet with a cairn-marked path that leads us up and over Barley Moor to the summit of Pendle.

Pendle Hill

The lion head of Pendle, with its tail resting in Pleasington and its fore paws gripping Barnoldswick, stands sentinel at the eastern portal to Lancashire. Inspiration to some and a curse to others, friendly and welcoming on a fine clear day, menacing and towering on those darker rainswept days, but always Pendle in all her moods. Legend, myth and fact have conspired to impress this hill deep in the Northern psyche, providing a Folk with an immortal image of these northlands.

The summit, 557m. above sea level (1827 ft.), is marked by a triangulation point that stands on the site of an old fire-beacon, which in turn is said to have been built upon an ancient burial mound.

Fire-beacons sited upon prominent hills are not uncommon in Lancashire and provided a quick way of spreading news of national or regional emergencies. The Pendle beacon has been used since Roman times up to the present day.

It was from this summit, in 1652, that George Fox had his great vision that moved him to found the Quakers, or Society of Friends, one of the earliest meeting places being sited at Twiston.

Towneley Hall Museum hold the major archaeological finds from the Forest side of Pendle, these include: a perforated stone mallet found at Newchurch, a gritstone axe-hammer with a polished surface found in Ogden Clough, a jadeite polished stone axe/adze and a Late Bronze Age socketed axe, both found on Pendle.

The view from the heights are magnificent — the Lakes, Bowland Fells, Ingleborough, Pen-y-Ghent, Malham Scars, the Aire Gap and the Pennine backbone all seem to gather round this most well known and loved of Lancashire's hills.

Pendle Summit to Well Springs Inn

From the Trig. Pt. walk in a NNE direction towards a metal gate in a crosswall, right and down to go over stile on left. Walk back up to the metal gate then bear to the right to follow a green track across the moor to pass over wall-stile (notice boundary stone built into wall on left marked with a 'D' — Downham, and bench mark). Follow a cairned path along the edge of the escarpment, past the stone wind shelter and on to the tall, well-built Scout Cairn.

From the Scout Cairn head over to the left to skirt the head of Mearley Clough and pick up a path that heads south-west across rough moorland to reach a broken wall. Pass over and continue on alongside the wall on right and on to the head of ridge. Follow the path down the steep descent to cross the stream by the iron post. Follow the clear path on, then across the slightly rising moor to head over to the left to join the road. Walk up the road to the Well Springs Inn.

Well Springs Inn to Wymondhouses

Walk up the road to pass over stile by gate on right and walk down the track to pass over next stile by gate. Follow old trackway down to Wymondhouses.

Wymondhouses

Wymondhouses is first recorded in 1285 as Wymotehuses, meaning 'Wigmund's House'. By the 14th century it had the status of a small hamlet. The farmstead we see today belongs to the 17th century, the sole survivor of the once tiny village.

Above the front door of the house is a tablet with the following inscribed upon it: Thomas Jollie Founded the First Congregational Church Here in

1667. Here in those days of religious persecution and the Five Mile Act, the Rev. Thomas Jollie, once minister at Altham until he was expelled in 1662, held services for those who broke away from the church and followed him.

In those days the barn served as a chapel (dated 1669 with the initials T.I. being those of Thomas Jollie); today the Jollie Memorial Chapel is sited at Barrow. Services were held in secret in the barn until the Act of Toleration of 1689, when the house was granted a licence for services. By all accounts Jollie was a hard man well known for his fire and brimstone speeches and sermons.

WYMONDHOUSES

Standing in the garden of the mullioned fronted farmhouse is a fragment of an inscribed stone tablet bearing the remains of some Biblical quotation. The tablet was originally set above the doorway of one of the now demolished houses at Wymondhouses.

Wymondhouses to Cold Coats

Enter farmyard and pass through the gate facing you by the cattle shed and walk directly on to cross Audley Clough via stile up into field. Cross the field on a right diagonal to pass through gate and walk on to enter Cold Coats via gate.

Cold Coats

Cold Coats, part of Great Mytton parish, contains one farmstead that itself contains many interesting features. Built into the gable end is a window from the Abbey at Whalley and the walls of the building contain many decorated fragments of masonry from the same source, and a shield bearing the initials T.W.A.

Cold Coats to Wiswell

Walk down the farm lane to roadway, left and on to go up Parker Place Farm driveway to pass through small gate at rear of house. On to the right to pass through gateway and on into next farmyard via stile by gate. Walk on to pass over two stiles then take the track up the hillside to enter field via gate. Walk on and up to far top corner of field to pass over wall-stile set in corner. Walk up and over to join a trackway by wood. Follow the trackway down to Wiswell.

Wiswell

The village of Wiswell grew up around an old spring, known in the 12th century as Wisa's Well or as some would have The Wise Woman's Well, in the southern corner of the ancient Reeves manor of Pendleton.

By the bank of the brook, below Wiswell Hall farm, stands Wiswell Shey Cross. This restored cross in an ancient socket is also known as the Weeping Cross. It marks the place of halt for funeral processions en route for Whalley churchyard from the outlying districts below Pendle and Clitheroe.

Wiswell Hall farm stands close to the site of the demolished Wiswell Hall. The drawing shows the Hall of 1669, home then of Thurstan Tomlinson whose datestone is now built into one of the farm outbuildings. A window from the old Hall is now built into the farmhouse.

"WISWELL HALL", HERBERT RAILTON

WISWELL HALL

The former Hall was the birthplace of the last Abbot of Whalley Abbey, the fiery John Paslew. In 1536 Paslew and the Whalley monks were implied to have been involved in a protest against the suppression of the lesser monastic houses, known to history as the 'Pilgrimage of Grace'.

The ill-conceived venture collapsed in October of that year. Abbot Paslew, some Whalley monks, along with the Abbot of Sawley, Thomas Bolton, and some of his monks, were tried for treason and condemned to death.

Paslew, with a Whalley monk named Haydock, together with a Sawley monk, Richard Eastgate, were hung, drawn and quartered at Lancaster. The remains of Paslew's body were brought back to Whalley to be displayed on the local gibbet.

The Abbey was seized by the crown and later sold in 1553, to Richard Assheton and John Braddyll, both engaged in the suppression of the rebellion.

Within the older Wiswell Hall was Paslew's private chapel. The font from

which can be found at the rear of the nave of Whalley Church. The Holy Water stoop from the chapel is today used as a baptismal font in Immanuel Church, Feniscowles near Blackburn.

A carved figure in stone of Abbot Paslew in prayer is built in above a window in one of the roadside cottages.

Vicarage House, the first one notices on entering the village from Whalley, is a good example of local architecture and contains within its fabric an older 16th century dwelling. During the 17th century this house belonged to Crombocks family of Catholic yeoman stock.

During those dark times the house, given its secluded position, became a place for secret worship and a number of hiding holes can be found in the house. The family remained Catholics until Dorothea Crombocks, the last of the family line, turned Protestant when she married the vicar of Whalley in 1665 — hence the house's present name 'The Old Vicarage'.

High Wall Well

High Wall Well is sited inside the ground of Bramley Mead Hospital. Covered by a grotto-type structure, the waters are reached by descending three steps. It is said to be the clearest and purest spring in the Whalley district, the only one that was never polluted.

Perhaps for this reason the Abbey monks laid leaden pipes from the well into their convent, sections of which have been located by the local History and Archaeological Society.

Wiswell to Clerk Hill/Spring Wood

Walk back up the lane to enter top field via gates and follow path on to enter the wood via stile. Upon leaving the wood walk directly on (the path over the stile on the left leads to Clerk Hill driveway and Wiswell Moor road) to pass over stile at Clerk Hill. Follow the path down to the edge of the golf course to return to Spring Wood Picnic Area.

Walk 8

AROUND
THE REEVE'S MANOR

Whalley, Standen, Pendleton,
Wymondhouses & Wiswell

10 miles, 5 hours

MAP: *O.S. sheet SD 63/73 PATHFINDER*

LUNCH: *Swan with Two Necks, Pendleton*

START: *Whalley Village*

Today we head west to pick up the Roman military way that will lead us to one of the oldest agricultural buildings in Lancashire. Leaving Standen Hey we head for the lovely village of Pendleton and discover her charms.

After visiting the hillside settlement of Wymondhouses we return by way of Wiswell and Clerk Hill to enter Whalley by old back lanes.

Riverside, valley floor meadows and hillside moorland make for many contrasts on this historic trail.

Whalley to Hardhill Cross/Roman Road

Walk down by the parish church and along The Sands to pass under the west gate of Whalley Abbey and on to enter Ridding Lane by a gate on the side of Cross House. This track leads us under the by-pass and past the water treatment works to the river bank. The path leads downriver then up to meet the iron railings of Calderstones Hospital.

Follow the track to the left around the hospital grounds to meet with Mitton Road. Pass over the stile on the left opposite and follow the path to pass over stile and stream. Walk directly on, passing the group of trees to Hardhill Cross.

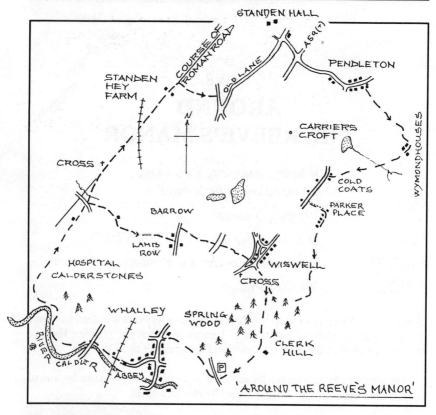

'AROUND THE REEVE'S MANOR'

Hardhill Cross

Between Mitton Road and Standen Hey can be found one of the most clearly defined sections of Roman roadway in this part of Lancashire.

By the side of the ancient roadway stands a monument known as Hardhill Cross, a large basestone with a square socket hole in the top. Though referred to as an 'ancient cross base', it is now held to be a socket stone plinth of a Roman milestone, recorded as such by the Lancashire Sites and Monuments Record.

At a point below Hardhill the Romans also erected a small bridge to carry the road across a stream. This consisted of two large slabs spanning the brook. Sadly, the bridge and much of the road surface have been destroyed by the landowner allowing motorcycle scrambles to take place in the fields around

HARDHILL CROSS
BY THE ROMAN ROAD

Hardhill, despite public footpaths and accessways along the 'scrambleways'. The destruction caused by this thoughtless act is irreparable, an act of gross vandalism. The vast majority of local farmers and landowners respect the near landscape and protect any ancient monuments in their trust, realising the importance of such monuments as a National Resource.

Thankfully the motor bike scrambling has now been stopped and the fields are now used for horse riding and jumping, a sport more sympathetic to the landscape.

Hardhill Cross to Standen Hey

Continue on to pass over stile by gate and on to cross the railway. Walk on along the Roman Road to enter the farmyard at Standen Hey via gates.

STANDEN HEY

Standen Hey

Sometime around 1140 the de Lacys established a corn mill between Henthorn and Siddows. This became known as Kings Mill when the lands around Clitheroe passed to the Crown and was leased out for a high rent.

Being the only mill on Crown property the miller had a monopoly on corn grinding in the district, a protected monopoly that existed until the mid 1800s. The mill's collection and distribution point stood alongside the Roman road at Standen Hey. Here, in Norman times, were built large barns and corn storage houses, and of the latter one still survives today (pictured previoius page), a multi-bayed building that would allow many carts to be loaded at one time.

Today the building, the oldest of its kind in Lancashire, stands in a ruinous condition awaiting a sympathetic restoration for use as a dwelling house. The other barns at Standen Hey are of a 17th and 18th century date.

It is no credit to any of us Lancastrians that we should allow this fine building to deteriorate and perhaps see its collapse. The Ribble Valley is the richest district in the county and it is my opinion that we should use the common purse to put this historic building into good order.

It would make a fine centre for rural crafts similar to the one at Hebden Bridge on the site of the old canal wharf. Buildings such as this are important in our long history, and we owe it to our children to preserve such heritage.

Standen Hey to Pendleton

Leave by the farm drive to go over stile on left of bungalow. Follow line of hedgerow on to pass over stile and along the raised pathway to the main road via gate. Cross the road and walk down to enter old road on the left via gate. Walk on to the junction at Standen Hall, right and on to cross the by-pass to follow the lane opposite to Pendleton.

Standen Hall

Standen Hall was originally built in the 15th century. The present structure is of the 18th century. The Hall has been home to the Aspinall and Starkie families.

Built into a wall at the rear of the hall is a stone tablet depicting the figure of a Roman standard bearer. This carved stone was found beneath the church at Whalley in the 15th century.

Height, 16½ inches.

Pendleton

Pendleton is first recorded in the 1086 Norman Survey as being one of four Royal vills within the Hundred of Blackburnshire, but its foundations go back thousands of years before that time.

The first settlement hereabouts was established during the later Bronze Age. Remains of one of their communal living huts were discovered at Carrier's Croft in 1968 during the building of a new house. An excavation of the site in 1975 revealed the circular nature of the hut which contained beneath its floor three collared burial urns.

The finds are now on display in Clitheroe Castle Museum along with a bone toddle and a small hollow cylinder of gold of Irish origin, the latter testifying to a long established trade route between Ireland and eastern England via the Ribble Valley.

During the Roman period historical analysis points to there being a villa or major farmstead being sited at Pendleton, possibly in the Standen district of the parish.

Later in the post-Roman, Celtic period Pendleton became the Head Reeve's settlement for the Whalley caput of the Cantrev (Hundred) of Blackburnshire, being a manor of two vills; one being estate/arable land, the other upland summer pasture, Pendleton and Huncoat respectively.

During the 13th century the manor of Pendleton was held by a branch of the Hoghton family, builders of the first Pendleton Hall. The later 17th century Hall is now a farmstead. The Hoghtons were followed by the Starkies of Huntroyde whose arms, a stork, can be found on the wall of Stork House in the village.

Upon glancing at the O.S. Pathfinder map of the area you will notice that all the field boundaries run parallel with each other, the fields being long strips. This pattern reflects the ancient medieval strips or doles that were farmed by the individual families of the manor.

Pendleton today is one of the best kept, prettiest villages to be found anywhere in Lancashire with a distinct air of antiquity.

By either side of the brook that runs along-side the main street are a number of 17th and 18th century houses. The one pictured here bears a date of 1693 with the initials I.I.T. being those of the Jollie family.

Central to the village is the local inn, The Swan with Two Necks, whose inn-sign pictures the said beast.

Some say that the pub is wrongly named

PENDLETON

and should be 'The Swan with Two Nicks', recalling the swan markings of old when swans belonging to the Guilds had their beaks marked to distinguish them from the Royal swans.

The inn is a favourite lunchtime and evening haunt for travellers and tourists in the Ribble Valley, offering a good range of fine ales, bar lunches and home made meals.

When wandering hereabouts at dusk I often call in for potato pie and peas and a few jugs of beer served in the most restful and pleasant surroundings to be found anywhere in this part of Lancashire.

Pendleton to Wymondhouses

Enter the farm track on the right just before the church and walk on to pass through stile by gate on right (notice the curious small building on the left. The steps provide entry for some creature, a hen house? But why the two chimneys?)

Follow stream up to go over footbridge. Walk up to the left and follow hedgerow on (white markers) to pass over stile by gate and on to pass over next stile by gate. Walk up to the left to enter Wymondhouses via wall-stile. Walk round to the front of the house.

Wymondhouses to Spring Wood Picnic Area

From the front of the farmhouse walk up the field to join old trackway via stile, then walk back to enter the further farmyard via gate. Walk on and pass through the gate at the end of the farmyard.

Now follow the directions given in the previous walk, 'Pendle, the Celtic Redoubt', to walk to Spring Wood car park.

Spring Wood Car Park to Whalley

Cross the main road and walk up to pass over stile in hedge. Walk down to the right to pass over stile to follow brookside path to the Manor House and Lawsonsteads via gate (see Whalley Village Trail for details on Lawsonsteads). Walk down Brookes Lane to Whalley.

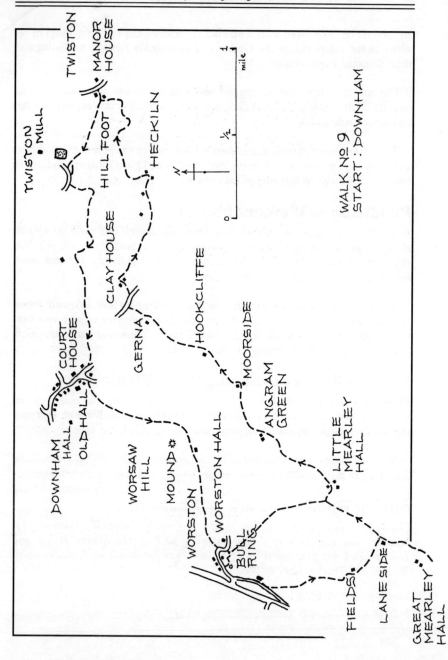

TWISTON

TWISTON MILL

MANOR HOUSE

HILL FOOT

HECKILN

CLAY HOUSE

N

0   ½   1
mile

WALK No 9
START : DOWNHAM

HOOKCLIFFE

GERNA

MOORSIDE

COURT HOUSE

DOWNHAM HALL
OLD HALL

ANGRAM GREEN

WORSAW HILL

MOUND

WORSTON

WORSTON HALL

LITTLE MEARLEY HALL

BULL RING

FIELDS

LANE SIDE

GREAT MEARLEY HALL

Oct '94

Walk 9

AMONG REEF KNOLLS HIDDEN BELOW PENDLE

Downham, Worston, Mearley and Twiston

9 miles, 5 hours

MAP:	*O.S. sheets SD 64/74 & 84/94 PATHFINDER*
LUNCH:	*Calf's Head, Worston*
START:	*Downham Visitors Car Park*

The folds of the landscape on the northern side of Pendle hide away a number of rustic hamlets and farmsteads. Amid these lower limestone knolls wildlife abounds, rural life is still rural life — no commuter development here where guinea fowl announce one's arrival and hare and deer dart freely. A walk that you will return to time and time again.

Downham

Nestling under the Lion of Pendle is the loveliest village of Lancashire, rural and unspoilt with village green and gurgling brook edged with stone-built cottages.

Thanks to the Assheton family, no intrusive television aerials/dishes, telephone or electricity cables exist here providing a lesson that planning officers should take good heed of.

The new information centre and car park is discreet, blending in well with village surroundings and a credit to Ribble Valley Borough Council who lead the field in their approach to tourism in Lancashire.

Downham Hall

The Assheton family have lived at Downham Hall since 1545, the present squire is Lord Clitheroe of Downham.

The structure of Downham Hall reflects a multitude of styles and periods. The 19th century main frontage hides the old Elizabethan hall of 1589. It has nine bays with a single storey portico of Tuscan columns. Around the corner the masonry indicates Elizabethan walls and 18th century windows.

On either side of the window above the portico are inserted ancient carved shields with the arms of Henry Lacy, Earl of Lancaster, and John of Gaunt, Duke of Lancaster. In the grounds are fragments of mediaeval masonry and a stone with the initials of Richard Assheton and the date 1589.

Near the entrance of the Hall grounds, a boulder known as the Great Stone protrudes from the wall. It is said to mark the grave of two Roman soldiers. The Roman Road between Ribchester and Elslack takes a major turn at Downham and the agger can still be traced in the nearby fields.

On the way round the limestone landscape of Worsaw look out for roe deer in the thickets, and especially look back on the knolls before entering Worston — natural scenery at its best.

Downham Visitors Car Park to Worston

After leaving the car park, walk up the farm lane on the right to pass over stile by gate. Walk on along line of fence, through gate and on passing Longlands Wood (home to a herd of Roe Deer) to pass through stone stile and on to end of wall. From here walk on, on a slight left diagonal, to pass through a stone stile in 'hidden' corner. Walk on to pass through next stone stile and follow the path around Worsaw Hill to pass through second gate on left above Worsaw End Farm. Pass through gate on right and follow brookside path, over four stiles and a footbridge onto track. Left and walk down the often wet lane to the roadway. Worston Hall is the first house on the left, the village and pub are along to the right.

Worston

With the construction of the Valley by-pass Worston has all but disappeared from view. Yet below Crow Hill it rests, as always, a rustic gem away from the maddening crowds.

Its hidden quality must have been also known to the Romans, one of whose number deposited 1,000 silver Denarii of the Higher Early Empire and a bronze lamp within an earthenware urn. The coin horde was discovered in 1778 by workmen employed in widening the road to Chatburn. The nine workmen divided the coins amongst themselves, but about 350 were recovered and given to the ladies of the manor and a Mr. Robinson. The earliest of the coins were those of Augustus.

Worston could well be the site of some Roman farmstead or station; the existence of the Worsaw Hill bowl barrow testifies to some form of settlement here in pre-Roman times.

An exploration of the village will reveal much of its ancient past. Behind the main street can be found a small meadow that was once the bull-baiting ring. In the centre of the meadow, hidden by the grasses is a large stone with a bronze ring to which the bull would be tethered. Wrestling and cock fighting matches were also held here and wagers taken upon the winners.

A farmhouse on the Downham road displays three stone heraldic shields above the porch doorway and a large doorhead in its garden wall. The first bears a lion rampant, the arms of Percy; the second is quarterly France and England; the third has on it three luces or pikes, the arms of Lacy.

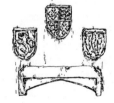

These fragments are all that remain of the old Worston Hall of Richard Greenacres, built in 1577 from the stones of Sawley Abbey. Richard's initials and a date can be found in the head of a narrow gateway to the side of the house.

The Greenacres were a powerful family around Clitheroe — landowners, MPs and governors of the Grammar School. They intermarried with neighbouring families, including the Asshetons of Downham Hall.

Worston Hall to Little Mearley Hall

Follow the direction of the footpath sign opposite Worston Hall, around the barn and over the stile. Follow line of wall on left up the field to go over stile. Walk on, on the same line past a lone tree to an earth banking. Here walk on a right diagonal to go over a stile. Follow right-hand fence up and onto the farm road. Turn left, then right to go up Little Mearley Hall driveway.

Worston to Great Mearley Hall

Pass through the village to take the left fork in the road. Walk on down the lane passing a house to go over stile by gate on left. Cross the field on a right diagonal to go over stile in hedge and cross the next field to go over stile in far corner. Cross field towards electricity pole to go over footbridge and follow stream up to go over stile. Cross the field on a right diagonal to pass through gate at far corner.

Follow farm lane up to pass through yard and on up the track to pass through gate. Follow fence line up to the track at Lane Ends (dated 1793 with the initials T.A.). Pass Lane Ends and walk down to Great Mearley Hall.

Great Mearley Hall

Only three huge earthworks remain of the once Great Hall at Mearley, along with a few old window mullions and carved stones that are to be found around the present farmstead.

In ancient times, the lands of Mearley, Little Mitton and Wiswell were held in demesne by the Deans of Whalley Church. These lands were granted for homage and service to Elias, son of Gamel the Fair (de Blundi) by Geoffrey, the Dean of Whalley (1193-1230). In the 13th century, Adam Nowell married the daughter and heir of Stephen de Mearley, and thus brought the Nowells to the Manorial estate of Mearley Magna.

The Nowells resided at Great Mearley for four generations until Lawrence Nowell exchanged, in 1364, the Manor and Chase of Mearley Magna with Sir Richard de Greenacres of Worston, for a moiety of the Manor of Read. This was the first settlement of the Nowells at Read, which remained their main family seat for more than four centuries afterwards.

Great Mearley Hall to Little Mearley Hall

Walk back up the lane to pass Lane Ends and on to turn right up Little Mearley drive to enter farmyard.

Little Mearley Hall

On approaching the farm one cannot fail to marvel at the splendour of the early 16th century bay window that originally came from the Abbot's house at Whalley Abbey; other carved Abbey stones can be found by the garden gate at the rear of the house.

A stone tablet above the large Tudor rear doorway bears the arms of the Nowell family quartered with those of the Walmsleys and the date, 1590, with the initials C.N. (top) and E.N. (bottom): Christopher Nowell who married Elizabeth, daughter of Thomas Walmsley.

LITTLE MEARLEY HALL

Little Mearley Hall to Hookcliffe

On entering the farmyard, go left between the barns to pass through a series of gates (higher) to follow wall on left to enter far field via gate. Walk on to go over stile by tall tree and water trough and walk on to pass over corner stile. Pass over the next stile and follow line of fence on left on and down to the right of Angram Green Farm (dated 1879 T.P.H.) to cross a stream.

Walk on to footpath sign and old lane. Follow 'Downham' FP sign up the driveway to Moorside. Pass through the farmyard by side of barn to go through gate and over footbridge. Follow trackway on, through gate and on up to Hookcliffe field gate on right, marked 'footpath'. Pass through gate to view south face of house.

Hookcliffe

Hookcliffe is a classic example of a Lancashire limestone and gritstone building. The limestone is usually unshaped, presenting a rough-hewn and uneven face. Gritstone has been used for mullioned windows, door sills and jams, fireplaces and corner stones.

On the east side of the house, to the left of the large chimney, is a stone with the initials R.A. and the date 1714. The low mullioned windows suggest an earlier date — the western section of the house being the oldest part. Notice the bricked-up doorway and window on the south face, this would have been the original entrance of the 16th century building.

Hookcliffe to Heckiln

Pass over stile at garden corner and walk down the field to follow track to the right towards Gerna Hill to pass over stile by gate. Cross the fields to pass over fence stile and on up by the wall to enter Gerna farmyard (1848 with initials of William Ashton). Walk down the lane to the road, turn right, then left up Clay House driveway to pass through the farmyard. At the rear of barn pass over stile on right and walk up the right of the field to pass over wall stile.

Walk to the left, over gully and on along the wallside for half its length to head up to the right to pass over wall stile onto farm lane. Walk directly on and follow fence to where it veers down to the stream. From here, walk over to the right to cross a stone stile above the stream. Walk up to the wall on the right of the barn and follow hollow-way to the right to enter Heckiln farmyard. Walk to front of farm.

Gerna and Clay House

These are two examples of later traditional building in the valley, their design recalling the Jacobean age much in keeping with other buildings in the area. One can only hope that modern builders will follow such a good example instead of erecting houses so out of keeping for their position in rural districts.

Gerna is a solid-looking farmhouse built by William Ashton in 1848. The windows are all mullioned with drip moulds above. Clay House is also of the same period and presents a regal face towards Pendle.

Heckiln

Heckiln is a substantial farmhouse with low mullioned windows and a stone slated roof built in c. 1600.

The origin of the name begs question. Is it from the old Norse 'Helkn' meaning 'barren, rocky ground' or could it mean 'high kiln' referring to the great limestone outcrop on this side of Pendle Hill? The 350 million years old seabed from the Lower Carboniferous Period provides a valuable resource for builders and farmers alike.

A mile south-east of the farm can be found the ancient Annel Cross that used to stand by the side of Four Lane Ends above Twiston. A guide stone nearby, erected in the 18th century, is said to have been made out of the shaft of the cross.

The last public hanging in the area took place at Annel Cross. Around 1840 a man was executed for stealing sheep and buried in the angle of the present north-west wall.

Heckiln to Hill Foot, Twiston

Walk back to rear of farm to pass through easterly double field gate and follow track down to pass through gate on the right. Cross the field in the direction of the modern barn on the opposite hillside to go over stile in short section of walling and on to go over next wall stile. Walk to the right and down by the wood to cross the fence and stream. Walk up the field to pass through field gate in wall and follow wall to the left to pass over wall stile.

Hill Foot Farm. c.n.

Walk on and enter Hill Foot farmyard and on past a row of three cottages to pass through stiles on up to the roadway at Twiston (not a village as such, only a telephone box and Royal Mail box).

Twiston, Hill Foot

The settlement of Hill Foot stands below the 'big end' of Pendle and is the centre of the manor of Twiston.

Hill Foot Cottages.

The run-down farmstead belongs to the 17th century and a number of mullioned windows remains on the south side and rear. To the north of the farm stands a charming row of cottages. The stepped windows of 'Yorkshire' style with the tiny porches make for a pleasing picture.

Above Hill Foot, beyond the road, stands the Manor House. This is a relatively modern structure, but the barn is interesting with a datestone above the door of 1757 with the initials J.S.

The stiles, gates and footbridges around Hill Foot are in a very poor condition and ought to be put in good order.

Twiston, Hill Foot, to Downham

Walk back down to Hill Foot farmyard to pass through bottom right-hand gate. Walk on along the brow of the hill to pass through gate and on down to cross the field to go over footbridge (notice Twiston Mill lodge down on the right). Walk over to the right, through old wall opening, then walk up the field to pass through gate in top right hand corner onto road.

Walk up the road to go through next gateway on left. Cross the field to far corner and follow trackway on to pass through gate. Follow right-hand fence on to go through gate and on along the track to the old quarry. Pass over stile on right and follow wall down to pass over stile by gate on left.

Follow line of hedge on to pass through old gateway then cross the field on a slight right diagonal to go over stile. Cross next field on a right diagonal to go over wall stile in far corner. Again cross this field on a right diagonal to pass over wall stile. Walk on and to the left to follow the stream down to the village.

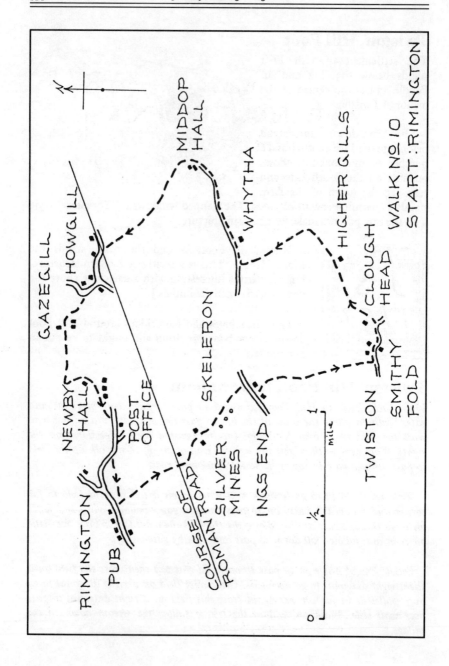

GAZEGILL

HOWGILL

MIDDOP HALL

WHYTHA

HIGHER GILLS

WALK Nº 10
START : RIMINGTON

CLOUGH HEAD

SKELERON

NEWBY HALL

POST OFFICE

SMITHY FOLD

TWISTON

RIMINGTON

PUB

SILVER MINES

INGS END

COURSE OF ROMAN ROAD

1 mile

½

0

Walk 10

A RAMBLE AROUND RIMINGTON

Rimington, Twiston and Middop

5 miles, 2½ hours

MAP: *O.S. sheet SD 84/94 PATHFINDER*

LUNCH: *Black Bull, Rimington*

START: *Post Office, Rimington*

On this walk we follow in the footfalls of the Roman legionaries who drove a road through these parts between their forts of Ribchester and Ilkley. The lands here have always been a border region, originally between the Celtic cantrevs of Craven and Blackburnshire and in more recent times between the West Riding of Yorkshire and Lancashire. A short walk it may be yet it holds many surprises.

Rimington

Rimington is mentioned in the Norman Survey of 1086 as a manor, and as a community it has grown little since those times. The parish is made up of the hamlets Stopper Lane, Howgill, Grazegill and Newby.

On the very edge of the parish stands the farmstead of Westby Hall. This was the site of a Lister family house known as "Arnold's Biggin". The Biggin or fish pond, from which the site takes its name, can still be traced along with a few remains of the Old Hall.

The composer of hymn tunes, Francis Duckworth, lived for many years in Rimington and named one of his tunes after the village.

Stopper Lane is the site of the disused lead mine which was reputed to have produced the silver for the 'Pudsay Shillings'.

Post Office, Rimington, to Black Bull, Rimington

Continue along the road and around to the right to leave by footpath sign on left by way of stile. Walk on to pass over next stile and follow right hand fence on to pass over stile on right near field corner. Walk over to the left, over stile then over to the right to road via small gate. Left, walk up to the Black Bull.

Black Bull, Rimington to Ings End

Return to pass again through small field gate and walk directly up the field to pass over fence-stile and on over the next field to pass over stile onto old lane. Pass through stile opposite and over to the left to pass over fence-stile onto old lane. Follow lane, over stiles to Hollins farm. Pass over stile by gate opposite and walk up the track to pass over stile on to the Silver Mines. Follow track on to pass over stile onto road. Walk down the road and over the bridge.

Ings End to Smithy Fold

Once over the bridge enter farmyard on left and go through gate opposite. Follow line of old hedgerow to go over fence stile. Cross field on a very slight right diagonal to go over stile. Pass over stile opposite and walk up the hill to go over stile by gate. Follow left hand fence, over stile, and directly on to go over stile by gate onto lane. Left, and walk up the lane to Smithy Fold.

Twiston

SMITHY FOLD, TWISTON

Twiston is a small parish consisting of the hamlets Higher Twiston, Ings End and Lower Gate. The name, in c. 1140 recorded as Twisleton, means 'the tun by the fork of the river'. The township stands between Ings Beck and Twiston Beck.

To the east of Lower Gate once stood a mediaeval chapel, now recalled only by the field name.

George Fox, founder of the Quaker movement, established a community at Twiston. Their now disused burial ground can be found at Red Syke Farm. George Fox is known to have had his revelation from God on the summit of Pendle Hill.

The oldest buildings in the parish are a 16th century farmhouse at Ings End and another of the same period at Hill Foot Farm.

Clough Head

Clough Head was once the home of the Twiston farmer William Bullcock who built the house in 1702 as is recorded by his initials and the date on the doorhead of the farm.

Twiston to Middop Hall

Walk on past Fern Side (dated 1798), Smithy Fold and the Bullcock Family Memorial into Clough Head farmyard. Through the gate, cross the field and over the stone wall stile. Cross the field to the far gate. Pass through the gate and follow track past higher Gills farm, on up, then left down to Whytha Road. Turn right and follow the road to Middop Hall.

Middop Hall

The old Domesday manor of 'Mithope' is one of the most extensive and valuable grazing farms in Craven and was part of the great possessions of the Boltons. It was later passed to the Lister family of Arnold's Biggin by marriage with a co-heiress of the Listers in 1312, during the reign of Edward II.

The name Middop means 'middle enclosed land'. Middop stands on the old borders of the Celtic Realms of Craven and Blackburnshire, and along with Bolton-by-Bowland formed a boundary march between these two areas.

Middop Hall is a 16th century house displaying mullioned windows with round-headed lights. Built into the wall of the barn are some architectural fragments from Sawley Abbey.

The Lister family of Middop were part of the great Yorkshire family whose seat for six centuries has been Gisburn Park. Their coat of arms can be seen in the east window of Gisburn Church. The family burial-place is on the north side of the communion table.

Middop Hall

Thomas Lister (1752-1826) was elevated to the peerage in 1797 by the title of Baron Ribblesdale of Gisburn Park. In the early 19th century he raised and equipped a troop of Yeoman cavalry of men from the surrounding district to fight in the Napoleonic War.

Middop Hall to Howgill

Pass through the farmyard and follow farm-road on, over the hill and down to large tree by fence corner. Follow fence down, over stile, on down to go over stream-bridge, then up and to the road via gate. Left, walk down to the road junction.

Howgill Manor House
J.O. 85.

Howgill

The road passing through Howgill is built upon the course of the old Roman Military road between Ribchester and Elslack. It was built in the 1st century as part of the cross-Pennine route to York.

To the north-east of Howgill are two earthworks. One is a small structure on Primrose Hill whose origins are unknown. The other is known as Bomber Camp and stands in a field to the east of Coal Pit Lane. The camp is square and surrounded by a ditch earthwork, its corners are on the points of the compass.

Within the enclosure have been found a number of Romano-British quern stones suggesting a native farmstead. The area must have been witness to the Roman campaigns against the Brigantes, a powerful con-

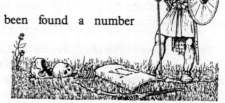

federation who were predominantly Bronze Age in physical type and social organisation. They were the numerically largest tribe in Britain.

Howgill stands between their two Iron Age hill forts at Ingleton and Colne, both constructed in the stormy 1st century when the North of Britain became openly hostile to the Roman yoke.

This was to lead to the Roman invasion of Brigantia (as Lancashire and Yorkshire was then known) by Cerealis 71/2 AD, and later the full invasion under Agricola in 79 AD.

Howgill to Newby Hall

Follow the road to the right and walk on to lone house to pass over stile by gate on left. Follow stream down, over stiles, to go over stile by gate at Beck Side farm. Pass through the farmyard to last building on left and walk on to the tree in corner of hedge. Follow hedgeside track on and over the field to enter Newby Hall farmyard via gate. Walk on to front of house.

Newby Hall

Newby Hall is now a farmhouse, much altered from the 17th century original; only the one-storeyed porch points to its earlier date.

Newby Hall

A path from the Hall leads northwards to William Rushworth's Field House, dated 1819. Over the door is a large stone tablet offering the following advice: "Repeat no grievances but study to be quiet and mind your own business". Obviously a man not given to small talk or gossip.

Newby Hall to Post Office, Rimington

Walk up past the Hall front following the road to a point where it bends to the left and pass over wall-stile. Walk on behind the greenhouses to pass over stile by gate onto road. Right, walk up to the Post Office (excellent steak and kidney pies, home made with solid chunks of meat, can be obtained here!).

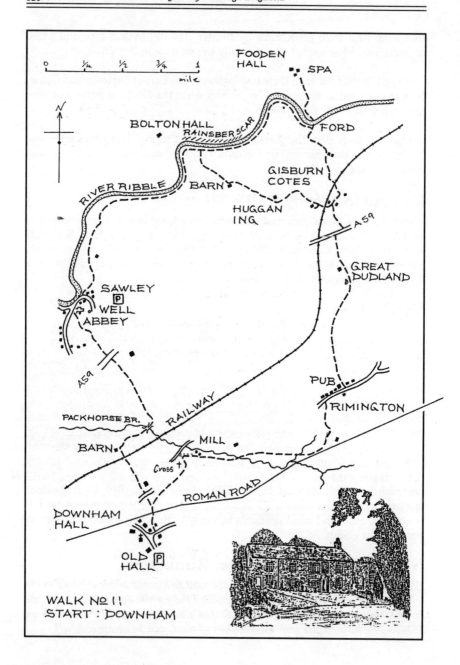

WALK Nº 11
START : DOWNHAM

Walk 11

A PILGRIMAGE THROUGH GRACEFUL ARCADIAN LANDS

Downham, Rimington,
Gisburn Cotes and Sawley

8 miles, 4½ hours

MAP: *O.S. sheets SD 64/74 & 84/94 PATHFINDER*

LUNCH: *Packed lunch & flask*

START: *Downham or Sawley Abbey*

What with Roman roads, an old water mill, wooded riverbanks, picturesque villages and a Cistercian Abbey — this walk has a great deal to offer. Every turn we take opens up new vistas of landscape so varied it will remain in the mind as a ramble to fondly remember.

Downham Village

The church of St. Leonard looks down on this calm and picturesque village. The church was established c. 1296, and has a tower of 15th century, the rest being of the early 20th century. The impressive tower has four bells, three of which are said to have come from Whalley or Sawley Abbey. They are known to have been in the tower since it was built. The three bells are inscribed thus:

1. 'Vox Augustini sonet in aure Dei'
2. 'Sta. Margareta ora pro nobis'
3. 'Sta. Katharina ora pro nobis'

The first two bells have the marks of John Walgrove c. 1408.

Opposite the church stands the village inn, once the George and Dragon, now renamed the Assheton Arms after the lords of the manor of that name. Across the road, beneath an old sycamore, are the village stocks where wrongdoers were placed in olden times.

Down the road, near the river, stands Old Well Hall, the manor house where the manorial steward lived. The Hall is a 16th century building with low mullioned windows and a projecting two-storey gabled porch, which formerly had a dated panel over the doorway. The building is now divided into three cottages.

The manor of Downham was part of the honor of Clitheroe, and in 1241 was held in dower of the Countess of Lincoln, widow of John de Lacy. The Dinelay family held it from 1354 till 1545, when it was sold to Ralph Greenacres, who in turn sold it to Richard Assheton in 1559.

The journal of Nicholas Assheton, a man fond of good sport and drink, written in 1617/19 , gives one a vivid picture of the life of a country gentleman in those times: "Eat, drank wine, was merry, and to the field again", sums up his life.

Nicholas's heir, Ralph, was a Parliamentarian during the Civil War, being placed on the committee for the sequestering of Royalist estates in 1643. A few years later, on the 15th August 1648, Oliver Cromwell's men were quartered at Downham on their way to the Battle of Preston. Ralph at this time was a Major-General and in command of all the Roundhead Forces in Lancashire.

During this period, the Second Civil War, he had in his command about 1,500 foot- and 1,200 horsemen. His Second-in-Command was Alexander Rigby, and in charge of half of the cavalry was Nicholas Shuttleworth, son of Richard Shuttleworth of Gawthorpe. After the Battle of Preston, Assheton's men cleared the north-west of Royalist garrisons, recovering possession of both Carlisle and Appleby castles.

Lancashire's militiamen played a vital role during both Civil Wars for which they were never fully rewarded, paid in short in arrears of monies owed to them. In such personal distress they disbanded, marking the end of an era for Assheton, Rigby and Shuttleworth.

The Assheton coat of arms can be seen above the door of the inn. It shows a fool with a scythe — apparently an ancestor feigned madness to escape from enemies — with the motto 'Nea Arrago Nec Dubito'.

Downham to Downham Mill

From the Post Office walk down Twiston Lane a short way to go up the green track on the left. Pass cottage front and go through gate to follow wallside path up, through stone stile and on to top of hill (you are now standing on the Roman road). Walk down the hill on a right diagonal to go between the limestone knolls and over the hedge-stile situated to the left of gate, onto Downham Mill driveway. Right, and walk on into the mill yard.

Downham Mill

The old Downham Corn Mill, that was running till the turn of the century, has been sympathetically converted into a very fine house. The position of the undershot water-wheel can be made out and the old grindstones make an attractive feature in the yard. Notice the mill pond and the water-race on the walk between the house and the weir, a true delight for the eye to behold.

Downham Mill to Rimington

Walk through the yard and over stile to follow old mill-race on to pass over corner fence-stile. Follow stream up to go over footbridge. Continue to follow stream up, over the rise and on to where a small stream meets it. Follow small stream up for 40 yards to cross and go over fence-stile. Walk up the hill on a left diagonal to go over stile on left of gates.

Walk down to go over stile near far corner of field. Walk on to go over next stile onto trackway. Left and go over stile by gateway. Walk up the field on a right diagonal, over old hedgerow, and on to go over stile onto roadway. Right, and walk on to the Black Bull at Rimington (Thwaites Ales).

Black Bull, Rimington, to Great Dudland

Pass over wall-stile on right of inn, left, on through gates and stile to farm lane. Pass through stile opposite and follow left-hand hedgerow, through gateway, and on down to go over footbridge and stile. Walk up to old hedgerow and on to pass over corner fence-stile. Walk across the field to far corner to go over stile, then pass through gate on left. Go over the fence-gate on right and walk on to pass over stile. Walk around the pond to follow sunken trackway on to Great Dudland.

Great Dudland

Great Dudland is a two-cell farmhouse of the late 17th century, previously the property of Lord Ribblesdale. Both south and north faces of the house retain most of the original character, it is a pity that the modern extension work is unsympathetic.

I find many old cheese-press weights on my travels, rarely coming across the complete thing. Here at Great Dudland is a complete press with weight and cross-marked base. The stones have, until recently, been used as a horse mounting block. In 1985 the present owner placed both stones at the front (once rear) of the house.

Also to be found at the front of the house is an ancient stone coffin that had previously been used as a water trough on the farm. This was brought from the Abbey at Sawley in the 1880s.

Great Dudland to Gisburn Cotes Hall

Walk down the drive to the main road. Cross the road and walk up to the right to go over stile in hedge on left. Follow left hand hedge down to enter next field and follow right hand hedge around to barn and Gisburn Cotes Lane. Left, over the railway bridge to Gisburn Cotes Hall.

You can now make your way to Sawley by way of Huggan Ing or by way of Fooden Ford, the latter being described first.

Gisburn Cotes Hall

Gisburn Cotes is a small hamlet consisting of a number of old farmsteads divided down its middle by the railway line. On the west side stands Gisburn Cotes Hall. The building has a centrally placed two-storeyed gabled porch.

Above the doorway is a datestone of 1659, and the window above still retains the original mullions. The rest of the house is of a later period. I suspect that the rebuilding was done with the advent of the railway.

Gisburn Cotes Hall 1659

The riverside path that we now take to Sawley is part of the recently recognised 'Ribble Way'. The path is well way-marked and has new solid stiles and footbridges.

Gisburn Cotes to Sawley via Fooden Ford

Walk back over the railway bridge and walk down the lane past the barns to go through gate on left at farm and on to cross the railway bridge. Follow left hand fence/hedgerow, through gates onto farm lane at Long Holme Row. Left, follow farm lane up to go through gateway on right at bend. Follow right hand hedgerow and old trackway to go over stile by old wall on right. Walk on to enter wood via stile and follow path along and down the steep banking to join the 'Ribble Way' footpath at Fooden Ford (only fordable when the water is very low). Follow the well-signed footpath down the river to Sawley. (Notice cheese press base built into driveway wall on left as you enter village).

Gisburn Cotes to Sawley via Huggan Ing

From the rear of the Hall pass to the right of slurry tank to pass through far right hand field gate. Cross the field to the top right hand corner to pass over stile. Follow right hand fence, on to go over stile, turn right into Huggan Ing. Go through the wooden five-barred gate on the left of the barn. Right, following wall to go through gate into the field. Cross the field on a left diagonal heading for the field barn. Go through the gate on the right of the barn and follow the right hand hedge down the field, over the fence and down to the river. Follow the Ribble Way well-signed path downriver to Sawley.

Sawley Abbey

The Cistercian Abbey of Sawley was founded in 1147, and was colonised from New-minster in Northumberland, which in turn had been colonised from Fountains Abbey in Yorkshire.

The Cistercians normally established their foundations on waste land in remote and uncultivated districts. In order to facilitate the task of forest clearance, marsh draining and agricultural overseeing they recruited cottars and small freeholders as lay brethren, opening up the religious life to classes hitherto excluded from it.

The great Cistercian houses of Northern England were greatly involved in the repopulation process following the 'Harrying of the North' by William the Conqueror during the period 1068 to 1070. Conversely there are instances where the monastic communities brought the destruction or movement of settlements, — examples of this are found mainly in middle England.

Tombstones at Sawley Abbey

The Abbey at Sawley was founded by William Barron Percy, grandson of the William de Perci who accompanied the Conqueror to England in 1066, and obtained from him large possessions in Craven.

At the Dissolution (1536/37) the community consisted of twenty one monks. William Trafford, the last abbot, like

PLAN OF SAWLEY ABBEY

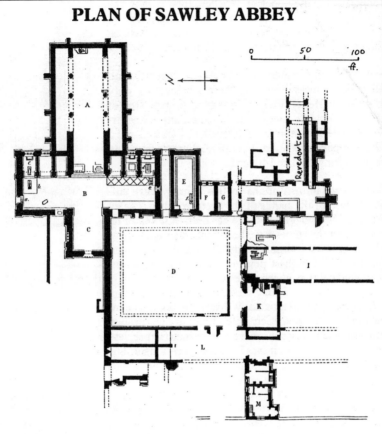

A. The Choir without Aisles, the Eastern Limb
B. Transepts, North and South Limbs
C. The Short Nave
D. The Cloister Court
E. The Chapter House
F. Sacristry or Vestry
G. Penitential Cell
H. Refectory and Day Room for the Monks
I. The Principal Refectory
K. The Kitchen. Notice the stone to receive one end of the horizontal spit
L. Lay Brothers Dormitory and Guest House
M. Detached building thought to have been site of the Abbot's House

ARMS OF SALLEY ABBEY.

John Paslew, the abbot of Whalley, took part in the monkish insurrection known as the 'Pilgrimage of Grace', for which he was tried at Lancaster Assizes, found guilty and executed on the 10th March, 1537.

After this the demenses of the Abbey, together with all manors, messuages, etc. thereto belonging, were granted by Henry VIII to Sir Arthur Darcy. One of the most notable monks of the community was Sir William de Rimmington, Chancellor of Oxford and a Great opponent of John Wycliffe, Lollardy's founding father during the late 14th century.

Few similar institutions in this country have suffered more in the hands of the destroyer than Sawley Abbey. The straggling village has been built out of its spoils, and the stones have been carried away as far as Gisburn, leaving simply scattered mounds and ruined masonry. The highest point of masonry is the south-west angle of the church nave.

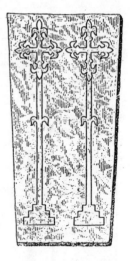

Tombstones at Sawley Abbey

The church had originally a straight-headed chancel, long transepts, each with three straight-headed chapels, and a very short nave — a curious feature, less long than it is wide. It was intended to be longer, but the poor community of monks could clearly not afford a greater building at the time.

An incongruous narrow north chapel was added to the nave in the 14th century, and during the early 16th century the chancel was widened and lengthened by way of aisles. Two old bread ovens built into a fireplace can be seen in a large piece of walling on the west facing the road.

The prominent arch used to straddle the roadway, but now acts as a decoration for a farmer's field gate; it is of no great interest being a folly built from Abbey materials by a local farmer in the 19th century. In the surrounding fields are many earthworks representing the agricultural and industrial enterprises of the Brothers, as well as fish ponds and water courses.

The village is a well-loved beauty spot, known for its pleasant riverside walks. Southport House is worth looking at; it has a similar doorhead as Key's Cottage in Bolton-by-Bowland, along with some inscribed stones from the Abbey built into the wall on the right of the doorway. The lintel is dated 1720. Over the river, in the garden of Bank Hall, are to be found more carved fragments from the Abbey.

The Spread Eagle Hotel is open for food and drink every day, with Table d'hôte and a la Carte Menus.

Sawley to Downham

Enter the Spread Eagle car park, opposite the front of the Inn, and walk to the rear to pass over the stile on right. Walk up the field on a slight right diagonal to go over a wall stile near a field gate. Walk on to enter lane via gate. Left, then over stile by gate on right. Walk up the old track, over stile and on to go over stile by gate.

Cross the main road and pass over stile by gate opposite. Cross the field to go through far gate. Cross the field on a right diagonal to go over stile. Follow left hand hedge, over stile and on down the field to go over a stile by tree. Walk down and cross the pack-horse bridge. Left, and over the wall stile on the right. Cross the field on a right diagonal to go over footbridge.

Walk up to the left to pass through gateway and on to walk around the wall to pass through gate at barn. Walk on to pass under the railway and follow the trackway up to the farm. Pass through the field gate facing you and walk up the field to pass through small gate onto roadway. Pass over stile opposite and follow the wooded path over the hill back to Downham.

> *The reverend pile lay wild and waste,*
> *Profaned, dishonoured, and defaced;*
> *Through storied lattices no more*
> *In softened light the sunbeams pour,*
> *Gilding the Gothic sculpture rich*
> *of shrine, the monument, and niche.*

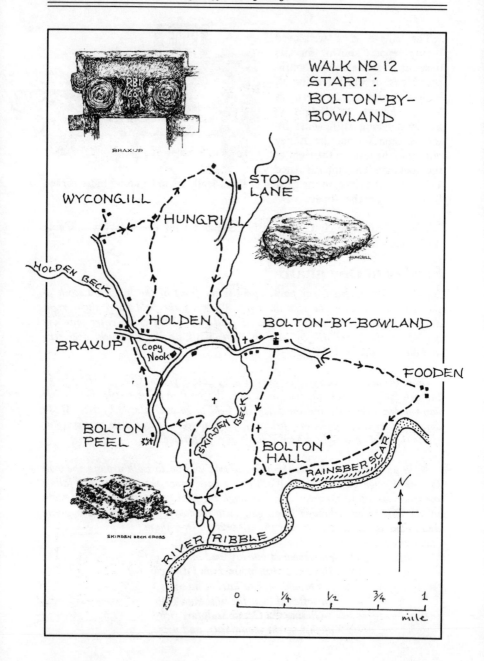

BRAXUP

WALK № 12
START :
BOLTON-BY-
BOWLAND

WYCONGILL

STOOP
LANE

HUNGRILL

HUNGRILL

HOLDEN BECK

HOLDEN

BOLTON-BY-BOWLAND

BRAXUP

Copy
Nook

FOODEN

BOLTON
PEEL

SKIRDEN BECK

BOLTON
HALL

RAINSBER SCAR

N

SKIRDEN BECK CROSS

RIVER RIBBLE

0   ¼   ½   ¾   1

mile

5/11/93

Walk 12

A KING IN RESIDENCE

Bolton-by-Bowland, Fooden, Bolton Peel,
Holden & Stoop Lane

6 miles, 3 hours

MAP: *O.S. sheets SD 64/74, 65/75, 84/94*
            PATHFINDER

LUNCH: *Copy Nook Inn*

START: *Bolton-by-Bowland.*

This walk takes us into a quiet and restful corner of the old West Riding of Yorkshire to discover the ancestoral seat of many great families: the Peels, the Boltons, the Pudsays and many of lesser weight.

We visit a church of which a King had a hand in the design, the site of an old Peel Tower from which one of our more famous Lancashire families take their name and a number of 17th century farmsteads.

The Copy Nook Inn at Holden is recommended for a lunch stop, the food, local produce, is prepared on the premises and the ale is very good. We suggest that you have a look around the village of Bolton-by-Bowland on returning from the walk.

Bolton-by-Bowland

Bolton-by-Bowland has the charm of a traditional Northern English village; a church on high ground and two village greens with a market cross, stocks and a pair of large millstones on the lower one.

The cottages are well cared-for and irregularly set along the main street and in the

KEY'S COTTAGE

centre of the village stands an old oak tree. One of the cottages has an unusual geometrical design on the doorhead which gives the house its name, Key's Cottage. It is dated 1716, with the initials I.R.M. The Coach House, Old Butcher's Shop and the Courthouse were built imitating Elizabethan and Jacobean architecture in the mid-19th century.

Dominant in the village is the Parish Church of St. Peter and St. Paul. A church is said to have stood here in 1190, but only the remains of a 13th century building can be traced; one lancet window at the west end of the south aisle, the priest's doorway and the re-used stones of the main south doorway belong to this period.

The tower is mid-15th century with diagonal buttresses and decorated battlements. On entering the church one will first notice the font. A solid octagonal piece bearing the arms of Pudsay, Percy, Tempest, Hammerton, Clifford and Bank.

Pudsay

Near the chancel is an impressive monument that marks the Pudsay tomb. Upon a slab of local Craven Limestone, about three yards long by two yards wide, are engraved the figures of Sir Ralph Pudsay, his three wives and twenty five children. Around the base of the slab are various coats of arms showing the descent of Sir Ralph and his second wife, Margaret Tunstall.

In the Pudsay Chapel is an early 16th century brass tablet showing two figures kneeling and facing each other. These represent Henry Pudsay, who died in 1520, with a tabard over his armour, and his wife, Margaret.

Above the main doorway is a stone with a sword

carved upon it, thought to be a memorial to one of the Bolton family of the 12th century. The church door is oak with 560 studs, most being square pegs in round holes. It is secured by a wooden bar that slots into the stonework and bears a date of 1705 on the outside.

On many of the pews are inscribed the date 1694 and the initials of their first owner, and in one case, the name of his property. The pews were arranged in their present uniform manner in 1886, the backs made to slope, the seats widened and the doors removed. Originally the pews were wider, some being square.

Bolton Church to Bolton Hall

Walk down the Hall driveway opposite the Church to the cottages and Hall stables. Notice the cross base on the way down, on the left before the bridge.

Bolton Hall

Within Bolton Park once stood Bolton Hall. It was demolished in ruinous condition in the 1960s. The bulk of the Hall was built in 1806, but at the rear was an outer stairway leading to a doorway, above which were battlements and a date, 1550. This would relate to an older house of the Pudsay family. Today only the stables and some old out-buildings remain. On the left bank of the driveway to the Hall is the base of an ancient cross.

Bolton Hall.

The manor of Bolton was held by the Bolton family from c.1129 until 1332, when upon the death of John de Bolton it passed to his grandson, John de Pudsay. The Pudsays remained at Bolton Hall till 1770, when Bridget Pudsay, the last of the line, died there.

Sir John Pudsay fought at Agincourt, and in the same year, 1415, his son Ralph was instrumental in capturing the Earl of Fife — enemy of Henry V. Ralph was knighted c.1448, and died in 1468 at 80 years of age.

Sir Ralph is best remembered for the hospitality he gave to Henry VI in the summer of 1464. A fugitive from the battle of Hexham (15 May 1464), Henry sought refuge at Bolton Hall and stayed for many months before moving on to Waddington and his eventual capture at Brungerley Hippings.

It is said, that Henry, described as "almost a professional architect", influenced the design of the church tower, which shows a higher order of decoration than the rest of the building.

Within the grounds of the Hall is an old well known as 'King Henry's Well' — said to have been discovered by the King using hazel divining. The Hall was once known to hold 'relics' of Henry's stay — a pair of jewelled gloves with gauntlets and linings of deerskin, a pair of soft leather boots and a wooden spoon. These can be seen pictured in Dr. T.D. Whitaker's "History and Antiquities of Craven". An examination was made of the relics in the 1930s and they were shown to be of the Stewart period, c.1600, and therefore not those of Henry VI.

Below the site of the Hall, overlooking the Ribble, is Rainsber Scar, known locally as 'Pudsay's Leap'. It is the subject of a legend going back to Elizabethan times; William Pudsay, the then Squire of Bolton, inherited many debts from his father, a recusant who died for his faith in York Castle in 1576. In such financial straits from the start, William had to resort to further borrowing, and it is from this that the legend grew.

Tradition has it that he coined silver from a mine on his estates at Rimington, these became known as 'Pudsay Shillings'. Upon hearing of their circulation, The Crown sent Revenue Officers to arrest the Squire. Warned of their approach, William mounted his horse, and with the officers in hot pursuit, forced his mount to leap the gaping chasm of Rainsber Scar, leaving the Revenue men without their prey.

William rode on to London, where he, upon arrival, sought an audience with the Queen, who was said to have been his Godmother. He was received and pardon was granted. The 'Pudsay Shillings', that seem to have come in times when creditors were most pressing, were more the result of further borrowing than that of mining silver.

William died in 1629, and was succeeded by his grandson Ambrose. During the Civil Wars, Ambrose was a Royalist and although only 14 years of age when the War broke out, commanded a Regiment of Foot. He was later forced into exile, having his estates sequestered by the Commonwealth.

After the Restoration he recovered his estates but found himself ruined being forced to sell the great majority of them. He sold Barforth estate in 1660 for £10,000. In 1667 he mortgaged Bolton Hall, and in 1668 his lands in Rimington were also mortgaged. Ambrose died in Ireland on the King's service in 1674 — death finally relieving him in his mid-forties of the responsibility of the families debts.

Those 130 years saw much troubled times for the Pudsays — a fate from which the family never recovered, penury never being far away. Today all is quiet and calm and deer roam freely upon the estates.

Bolton-by-Bowland to Fooden

Leave the village along the Gisburn road, past the church and on up to pass through gate-stile on right by farm lane. Walk on, following the old tree line to go over stile by gate near short section of walling and on to pass over stile at right hand end of wood. Walk down the field towards the farm to enter Fooden via gates. Fooden Hall is at the bottom of the farm lane.

Fooden Hall

In the most unlikely places one can stumble upon an absolute treasure — the tiny hamlet of Fooden being such a place. Hidden from the casual eye by Moorfield plantation, one can hardly believe that such a delightful nook could really exist. One cottage has an array of dove-cotes set into the gable of the porch, adding an air of tranquillity to an already arcadian abode.

The grandest is the 17th century house of Fooden Hall. It has a centrally placed two-storeyed gabled porch with a round-headed doorway on moulded responds. Above the doorway is a six-light mullioned and transomed window. All the other windows are mullioned with drip-moulds above. Inside the Hall is a huge stone fireplace — just the thing for a cold winter's evening, watching the embers glow in a glass of mulled ale.

At an angle in the garden wall is a stone trough known as Fooden Spa, a sulpher well that emits a medicinal water, said to have an excellent effect. The water runs down a small gully, then disappears to finally percolate, in a much diluted state, through the roof of Arthur's Cave.

The cave can be found 200 yards downriver from Fooden near the loop in the Ribble called Denham Wheel. It has the length of 100ft and contains numerous rockfalls. A left-hand passage round the first fall meets a stream which can be followed past various collapses to a final choke. This Grade I cave is also known as 'Otter's Den'.

Fooden to Bolton Hall/King Henry's Well

Walk back up the farmyard, through gate to go left around the barns on to track to go directly on and over stile. Follow left-hand hedgerow, over stiles, and on down to pass through gateway. Follow right-hand fence on, through second gateway to follow fence down to go over stile and stream. Cross the field directly to go over fence stile and on to go through gateway on to farm lane. Right, and walk on to go right at Bolton Hall farm buildings. Follow lane up to go left through ornamental gates and on down, past the hen houses, to two small decorated gate-posts. King Henry's Well is over on the left.

Bolton Hall to Bolton Peel

Follow curved wall on the right and down the track to go through gate. Cross the field directly to ford the stream (the footbridge was washed away) and on to find footbridge on left of banking — DO NOT GO OVER FOOTBRIDGE. At footbridge stile, go right and follow path up to go over fence-stile. Follow right-hand fence to end of trees, then cross the field on a left diagonal to go through kissing gate near stone gateposts. Walk on, following far right-hand fence to go over corner stile. Cross the field on a left diagonal to go over stile and on to go over footbridge. Walk directly up the hill to go over wall-stile to Bolton Peel.

Bolton Peel

The 17th century farmhouse at Bolton Peel displays many fine mullioned windows and a gabled porch of a good size. The porch door is constructed of a number of stout oak boards pegged together and swings on a pair of robust wrought iron hinges, all secured by a massive lock. Behind the door, two recesses, one in each jamb, accommodate a large oak bar which would be slid into position at night.

The old barn on the side of the road is of cruck construction. It is well worth having a look inside — with the owner's permission.

Outside the front gate stands a preaching cross set in an ancient base. It is one of four that can be found within the area of Bolton-by-Bowland. The cross is similar to that standing in Clapham village by the river.

To the west of the farmhouse, just within Spring Wood, can be found the remains of an ancient moat. Here once stood a Peel Tower surrounded by a large ditch. A Peel was a mediaeval fortified tower that provided a retreat in unsettled times, the family usually residing at another place, in this case it would be Bolton Hall.

The farmstead is also known as Bow Laithe, and is the ancestoral home of the Peel family, early East Lancashire industrialists who gave England a Prime Minister in 1841.

Bolton Peel to Holden

Walk down the road to go over a stile in the bend of the road. Cross the field to go over a stile by the river. Follow the riverside path to Holden, Braxup is on the left. If lunching at the Copy Nook, follow the road back to Bolton-by-Bowland to find the Inn at the junction.

Braxup Farmhouse, Holden

Holden is a pretty hamlet seated on the banks of Mear Gill, a rapidly streaming brook that joins the Ribble at Sawley.

Braxup Farmhouse is outstanding with its whitened walls and black painted window stones. Above the front door is a datestone with the initials R.B.I. and the date 1687. The drip moulding continues above the ground floor windows. The two upper windows are, as at Higher Heights, of that unique design originating in the West Riding. The barn is dated 1676 with the initials R.B.

Holden to Hungrill

Take the right fork at the road junction and walk up to go up steps at gap in wall on the right. Over the stile and follow hedge to go through gate. Follow right-hand hedge to go over stile. Walk around the brow of the hillside and follow line of old hedgerow up to go through gate and on to Hungrill.

Hungrill

Hungrill is a large three-storeyed
building of the late 17th century.
With its numerous out-buildings it
gives the appearance of being a mill
rather than a beckside farmstead.

What makes the site even more intriguing is the presence of the great
circular stone that sits at the side of the house. The stone once covered the
nearby well with steps leading to it. In the round hole was positioned a water
pump and the grooves allowed the surplus water to run away to the sides.

Hungrill Barn sports a fine Gothic-style doorhead dated 1699, that I take to have come from
the farmhouse some time before the side porch was
added.

Hungrill to Wycongill

*Follow overhead lines to go over stile on right of house. Turn right and walk
up the lane to Wycongill.*

Wycongill

Wycongill presents a symmetrical frontage of mullioned windows with a
central gabled porch. The whole belonging to the first half of the 17th
century. What a pity that the stonework has been subjected to coats of cement
render.

The site is first recorded in 1302 at Wykingile, a name of Scandinavian
origin meaning that it was once a cattle/dairy farm.

Upon the south-west heights above the farm are the remains of the old Victoria lead mines that were last in production in the 1870s, the well-rutted miners' tracks can be made out, leding over the hill to follow the old Rodhill Track to Sawley.

Hungrill to Stoop Lane

Walk past the barn to go through the left-hand gate. Follow right-hand hedgerow/fence to go through a gate. Walk up to corner in fences. Cross field on a slight left diagonal on to farm lane to ford brook. Walk up past farmhouse to turn right by the last shed to go through a gate and over a stone stile. Walk up the field on a left diagonal to go through a gate on to the road. Stoop Lane is the house opposite.

Stoop Lane

Stoop Lane stands on the old road between Tosside and Bolton-by-Bowland, remarkable for its dominant and squat porch. Above the wide doorway is a tablet with a date of 1701 and the initials R.T.M. and above this an upper window of the same type that we find at Braxup and Higher Heights.

The building has recently been restored and the final product is a delight to the eye. Our thanks go out to its owner and his workers.

Stoop Lane to Bolton-by-Bowland

Walk down the road to go over stile on left by sign "Oaktree Nurseries" and follow fence. Over stile and straight along the field about 60 yards left of power line to small gate. Follow the river down over next two stiles to Bolton Bridge. Left and walk into the village.

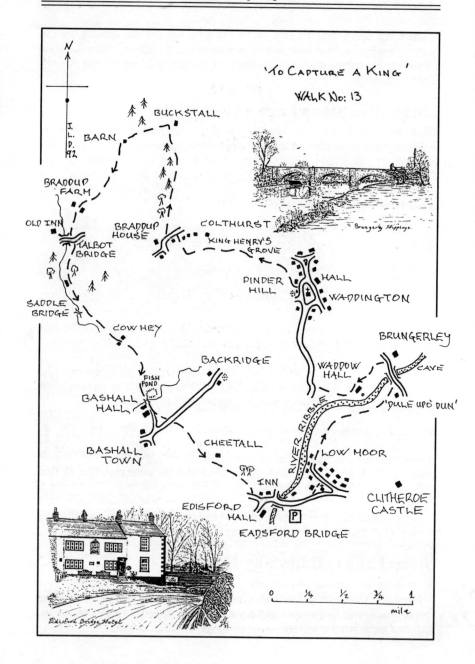

N

J.
L.
D.
92

BARN

BUCKSTALL

BRADDUP
FARM

OLD INN

BRADDUP
HOUSE

TALBOT
BRIDGE

COLTHURST

KING HENRY'S
GROVE

'To Capture A King'

Walk No: 13

Brungerly Stippings.

SADDLE
BRIDGE

COW HEY

PINDER
HILL

HALL

WADDINGTON

BRUNGERLEY

CAVE

BACKRIDGE

WADDOW
HALL

FISH
POND

BASHALL
HALL

'DULE UPO' DUN'

BASHALL
TOWN

CHEETALL

LOW MOOR

RIVER RIBBLE

INN

EDISFORD
HALL

P

CLITHEROE
CASTLE

EADSFORD BRIDGE

Edisford Bridge Hotel

0   ¼   ½   ¾   1
                        mile

Walk 13
TO CAPTURE
A KING

Clitheroe, Waddow, Waddington,
Talbot Bridge and Bashall Hall

8 miles, 4½ hours

MAP: *O.S. SD 64/74 PATHFINDER*

LUNCH: *Lower Buck Inn, Waddington*

START: *Eadsford Bridge Car Park*

For the casual and regular visitor to Clitheroe this walk gives one a little taste of the district's surrounding charm and hidden delights.

Waddington and Eadsford Bridge are popular stopping places for day trippers, yet concealed close by are enchanting microcosms of rural life thankfully secreted and preserved from the rude intrusion of the 'Madding Crowd'.

Eadsford Bridge

The bridge is a medieval stone structure and the original ribwork can still be seen under the central arch. In the 1300s tolls were taken for pontage (carriage of goods across the bridge) from traders using the Lancaster-Clitheroe medieval way. The bridge was also the site of a battle some 850 years ago.

In 1138 King David of Scotland led his army on a raid into England. He detached part of his army into Yorkshire under his nephew, William fitz Duncan. With great carnage they laid waste the monastery of Furness and the province of Craven with fire and sword.

On the 10th June that year William was attacked by the forces of King Stephen at Eadsford Bridge. William routed this force and much blood was spilt by his men, forever staining the fields of Edisford with the quartered bodies of the King's men. This raid also penetrated into Coupland where Calder Abbey was plundered and its inhabitants put to the sword.

Old charters tell as that William fitz Duncan had already acquired the district north of the Ribble at Edisford along with Skipton in Craven by his marriage to Alice, one of the co-heiresses of William Meschin, the brother of Rannulf, Earl of Chester.

This being the case it seems likely that he made the attack because he was being forcibly kept out of his inheritance. Or perhaps he had a private feud with his neighbour, Ilbert de Lacy, lord of the honor of Clitheroe, who also held lands in Craven.

The battlefield has now given way to more pleasant pursuits. An indoor swimming pool, pitch and put course, children's playground, an excellent caravan and camping site and a miniature railway all provide a splendid amenity for visitors to the district. The riverside path down to Siddows provides exercise for the motorists' legs.

The hotel across the river is the Edisford Bridge Hotel and provides bar snacks and evening suppers. The pub sign depicts the sturdy bridge, and the seats below permit the weary traveller to rest his legs.

Edisford Bridge Car Park to Brungerley Bridge

Leave the car park and cross the road to walk past the front of Ribblesdale Pool and on over the playing fields to the roadway at Low Moor. Follow road to the left, then right to go right at fork (Ribble Way sign) past the old Wesleyan School (1866) to pick up trackway.

Walk on past the allotments and on to pass over stile. Follow wallside path to go over next stile. Follow line of fence on to corner and cross the field to pick up descending pathway above the weir(Waddow Hall now in view). Walk down to riverside and on to pass over stile. Walk on to Brungerley Bridge.

Brungerley Bridge

Brungerley Bridge is one of many bridges that before recent boundary changes used to link Lancashire with Yorkshire, as a stone set into the bridge tells us. In the days before the bridge was erected people crossed the Ribble by way of hipping stones set into the bed of the river. These were sited above the modern bridge.

These stones were fraught with danger, due to the narrow channel between rocks forming a deep, slowly circulating whirlpool. Many an unfortunate traveller has met their end whilst traversing the swell. The legend of Peg o' Nell originated here (see below). It was she, it claims, who took the victim to the watery depths of the river.

Local folklore tells us of an old inn that once stood near Brungerley. The inn was known as 'Dule upo' Dun' from its sign representing the Devil galloping madly along upon a dun horse.

Legend holds that a poor tailor of the district sold his soul to Satan in return for riches. However, when finally the moment of his damnation came, the Devil repented and allowed the tailor one more final wish.

The poor tailor seeing a dun horse standing close by wished that his greatest enemy should be carried of to hell upon the steed's back. The Devil granted him his request, mounted the horse and rode furiously away, leaving the tailor to be thankful of his good wits that prevailed over his original greed.

Henry VI would remember Brungerley for quite different reasons. After the Battle of Hexham, the luckless Henry found his way to the Bowland district, seeking refuge first at Bolton-by-Bowland and later at Waddington. Whilst staying at Waddington Hall he was betrayed and later captured by John Talbot of Salesbury and others in 1464.

They assaulted the Hall, but the deposed king escaped. A little later, whilst crossing the Ribble by way of Brungerley Hippings, he was overtaken and captured on the Lancashire side of the river, less than a mile north of Clitheroe Castle. He was thence carried bound to a horse to London and imprisoned in the Tower.

Kept in the farmhouse at Brungerley is the figure of a woman carved in oak. Sadly the figure was slightly damaged by a barn fire some years ago, but thankfully rescued by the farmer. Upon examination the figure shows to have been once brightly painted. The style of costume and headgear depict a woman from the medieval period — St Helen, wife of Constantine?

Brungerley Bridge to Waddow Hall

Cross the bridge and follow road up to enter grounds of Waddow Hall at footpath sign.

Waddow Hall

Look at Waddow Hall on the opposite side of the river — was ever a house situated on a site more beautiful than this? It is transcendently handsome, lying as it does at the foot of an eminence covered with trees which completely shelter it on three sides. To the front is a fine sloping lawn, at the bottom of which the Ribble dashes.

The house was originally built in Tudor times as a dower house for the Tempest family. In 1267, the name of Roger de Tempest of Bracewell occurs in the Assize Roll as Lord of Waddington. It was he who founded the parish of Waddington and paid a priest to hold service there.

The lands remained in the Tempest Family until 1657, when the last of the male line, Richard Tempest, ruined the estate through his great extravagance. Richard cared more for the life of a dandy than that of a farmer, gambling and drinking his way through the family fortunes. This path was to lead the foolish fellow to the Debtors Prison on whose rat infested floors he was to meet the grim reaper.

The oldest part of the house is enclosed within the present building. This older building is shown on an oil painting of 1690. Painted in oils on a wooden card table. It now hangs in the entrance hall below the main stairs. The Tudor house is now completely hidden behind the Jacobean hall. But the oak-beamed rooms, still in use as bedrooms, date back to the earlier building.

Waddow Hall from the card table painting dated 1690, depicting that era

In the grounds of the Hall is a spring known as Peg O'Nell's Well. By the side of the well there is a headless statue said by some to be a likeness of Peg. Tradition has it that Peg was a serving maid at Waddow who fell in love with the eldest son of the family, greatly offending her mistress who expressed a wish that Peg would fall and break her neck.

In reply Peg stated that if she did succumb to such a fate she would place a curse upon Waddow — every seventh year the River Ribble would claim a life, though not necessarily a human life. One day Peg slipped on the ice around the well and the malediction was fulfilled. When 'Peg's Night', the last night of the seventh year, came round, unless an animal was drowned, some human was certain to fall victim of the curse.

The figure by the well holds in one hand a sceptre and in the other a book. It is similar to a statue of St. Margaret of Scotland. Peg is short for Margaret and Nell is short for Helen, patron saint of the parish church of Waddington. Perhaps between the two is held the mystery of the statue's identity.

The Girl Guide Association purchased Waddow Hall Estate in 1928, and it is now used as a Commonwealth Training Centre. The drawing above shows the Tudor Hall and is featured in the Guides' handbook of Waddow.

The head of the figure is kept inside the Hall.

Waddow Hall to Lower Buck Inn, Waddington

Follow private road to cattle-grid near rear of Hall. Here follow footpath on right up around the Hall to pass over double stile on to a trackway. Follow trackway to the main road. Turn right and walk along the road to the Lower Buck Inn.

The Buck Inn

Buck Inn

The Buck Inn, dated 1760, is one of the few remaining examples of a true country inn. The landlord serves a good selection of fine beers and ales to be quaffed by an open fire and good talk can be had without the tinny interruptions of an over-amplified juke-box, as is the case with many public houses today.

By a wall at the bottom of the inn's cobbled entrance stands an old horse mounting block, a reminder of an older way of travel.

Pinder Hill Bronze Age Burial

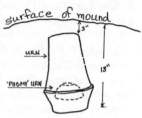

To the south-west of the Buck Inn stands a hillock of glacial debris known as Pinder Hill. A small mound on the summit of the rise was excavated in 1887 and yielded a Bronze Age burial urn. Inside the urn, which was inverted, was a mass of broken and partly calcinated bones, more than half filling it.

POSITION OF URNS WHEN FOUND

Within this mass was found an 'incense cup/pygmy urn', two worked flints and a worked bone object. The presence of an 'incense cup' is thought by some to mark a female burial, the openwork pattern indicating basketry being particularly the work of women. Yet given the inverted position of the large urn the smaller may have been merely a stopper and may have no other significance.

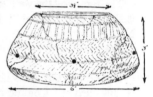

The flints are of the type used for the preparation of skins and preparing thongs of hide. The bone object is a toddle used to fasten a coat or other. These finds are now on display in Clitheroe Castle Museum.

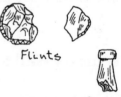

Flints

Bone

Bronze Age axes have been found at Up-Brook Farm, Waddington, and the horn of an 'auroch', extinct during the Bronze Age, in the Ribble at Low Moor.

St Helen's Church, Waddington

A church dedication to St Helen can often point to a post-Roman British population. Helen was the mother of Emperor Constantine, and was said to have been born in Britain. The dedication continued to be popular into the High Middle Ages. The

Parish Church of Waddington was established by Roger Tempest in 1267, who also paid for a priest to run the parish.

Of the early foundation nothing remains. The tower is the oldest part of the church, being erected in 1501. The font is probably also of that time. The

as a ruin in 1815.

benches in the Browsholme Chapel are Late Stewart, and well worth a look at, being the most distinctive in the church.

The reference to Wada, an Anglo-Saxon chieftain, both in the church and on the gateway of Waddington Hall, must be treated with a large dose of salt. The story owes much to John Waddington, restorer of the Old Hall, a great romantic and benefactor of the church. His story goes that after the Battle of Billington, 796, the defeated Wada settled here with the remains of his army. The settlement grew and was known as Wada's Tun.

Mr Waddington thought himself to be a descendant of that ancient chieftain, a whimsy one can allow him in view of his good works in the village. In truth the name Waddington is of Anglo-Saxon origin, 'Place of the Waddow Folk'.

An excellent History and Guide, by Nora Mary Goodchild, is available from the church. It covers all aspects of the building with further notes on places of interest around Waddington.

Waddington Hall

The Hall was restored by John Waddington in 1901. The present building is obscured from the road by a high wall and tall trees, but a path runs by the side of the Hall giving a view to the rear. The greater part of the pre-Reformation building is still in existence. The original walls and windows can still be seen in the Great Hall, and the Monk's Room is also of the same early period.

In fact the Monk's Room may be even older; some say that it dates back to the 11th century. The reason for the name is obscure. It has been suggested that the name arose because the room was used by monks travelling between the abbeys of Sawley and Whalley. Others tell of the Black Monk of Abingdon who is said to have betrayed Henry VI to the Talbots of Bashall Hall.

Behind the panelling in the Great Hall is the entrance to the 'secret staircase' leading to a spacious room above known as the 'King's Room'. A modern carved cupboard shows pictures of Henry's attempted escape — up the staircase to his bedchamber, down a ladder to the ground, and across the fields to Brungerley where he was captured on the Clitheroe side of the river.

The poor fellow's name still lives on in the district, a King Henry's Grove is marked on the Ordnance Survey map. Until a few years ago there was a small cave in Brungerley Park. Named King Henry's Cave, this may have been the site of a hermits' shelter (the changing course of the river has now obliterated all traces of the cave).

A Hermits' Chapel of St. Oswald was known to exist in the Waddington district around 1444. It was common in those days for hermits to assist travellers across rivers, and the cave would have provided the hermit with some shelter. As to the site of the old chapel nothing is known. It may have stood by the old well in the grounds of Waddow Hall.

In the rear garden of Waddington Hall are to be found two low burial mounds, which are said to date from the 9th century.

Waddington to Braddup House, Colthurst

Take the lane behind the Lower Buck and after a few yards turn up the driveway on the right (footpath sign), pass the house to go through white gate. Cross the stream and over wall-stile and follow path on to go over next wall-stile. Bear left across the field to corner of wire fence. Here, keeping the fence on your left, walk on to go over fence-stile. Follow right-hand hedge to pass over stile below Hollins Farm. Cross the field to pass over a stile.

Right, walk on then down to the left to go over bridge and pass through left-hand gate. Follow fence on to go over stile. Follow right-hand hedge to gated trackway. Here, walk over to the left and go over footbridge. Cross the field directly to go over stile by stone wall.
Follow lane to the left a short way to go through small gate on right. Walk up the field, with the farm on your right and the clump of trees on your left, on to go over a woodside stile. Follow path through the wood to roadway via gate. Left, walk down to Braddup House on the bend of the road.

BRADDUP HOUSE

Braddup House

Here we have a fine old farmhouse of the late-Stewart period, though the present building is much restored. I like the innovation of the rear stairwell windows. A datestone can also be observed on the front of the building.

Facing Braddup House is the entrance of Whinny Lane, an old trackway between Backridge and Waddington Fell. The lane is mostly overgrown now, providing a natural habitat for many types of wildlife. Wood mice scurry around, hare look to and fro and pheasant seek refuge from the barbarian's gun. All in all a nature lovers paradise.

Braddup House to Talbot Bridge

At the foot of Braddup House driveway notice a field gate on the right. Pass through the gate and on to enter wood. Follow overgrown bridleway up through the wood to pass through gate on to farm lane. Right, through gate, then go left up the edge of the field (good view of Pendle over to the right), over stiles and on to pass through field gate. Walk on to pass through next gate and follow left-hand fence, then wall to meet with farm lane via gates.

Pass through gate on left to follow right-hand fence on, through three gates to the ruin of Burbles Hill Barn. Walk around the back of the barn and cross the field on a left diagonal to the end of the far hedgerow to step over stream and over stile. Cross the field on the same left diagonal to go over stile by gate. Follow right-hand fence on to enter Braddup Farm yard (spaniel dogs will herald your arrival). Pass through farmyard to front of house. Walk a few yards down the farm lane to pass through field gate on right. Follow overhead cables to brook and walk downstream to Talbot Bridge via gate.

Talbot Bridge

Talbot Bridge straddles an old track linking Bashall Hall with Browsholme Hall. The track can still be made out running alongside the field path above Cow Hey on through Rugglesmire and Clough Bottom to pass over the 16th century arch of Talbot Bridge and on to Browsholme.

Notice the 17th century carved stones telling us why and how the bridge was erected. The farmhouse standing near the bridge was once the Woolpack Inn, giving a clue to the travellers' trade in those bygone days.

Talbot Bridge to Saddle Bridge

On coming out on to the road, turn left and walk up for forty yards to leave by a stile up on the right at end of wood. Follow the right-hand fence down to pass through field gate. Follow old hedgerow down to pass through next field gate near farm. Follow track to the left to pass through gate. Saddle Bridge is over on the right.

Saddle Bridge

Upon finding Saddle Bridge the eyes are greeted by a veritable fairyland. What tales could people tell of the folk who have oft crossed this enchanting bridge! Nestling in an idyllic setting the bridge rises like a huge stone saddle over the water.

It is said that kind fairies erected the bridge in a single night, having taken pity on an aged woodcutter who was being sorely tormented by a witch who lived near another crossing further upstream.

Saddle Bridge to Bashall Hall

Follow the stream down some way to meet with an old hedge-lined track, then follow fence running alongside on the right of the track to go over stile. Follow line of fence on to enter Cow Hey farmyard (yelping dogs, but chained up). Pass through farmyard and follow the lane on down to Bashall Hall.

Bashall Hall

Bashall Hall was built by the Talbot family and is an uncommonly curious and impressive house. Constructed over many periods, Early Georgian and Elizabethan stand side by side.

The whole is surrounded by walled gardens and accessory buildings. One of these buildings, an Early Georgian Summer House with large vases on top, brings a touch of Versailles to Bashall.

The drawing pictures the old barracks of the Talbots' retinue of troops. Much half-timbered work still remains, and on the other side a wooden gallery runs the length of the first floor. Looking up one almost expects to see a trooper polishing up his boots or putting a shine upon his breast-plate, so good is the restoration work.

It was from this Hall that John Talbot of Salesbury, his cousin Thomas Talbot, son and heir to Sir Edmund Talbot of Bashall, and Sir James Harrington set out to effect the capture of King Henry VI, who was in hiding at Waddington Hall.

In the tumult of the Wars of the Roses many local families were torn as to where their loyalties lay — should they support the deposed Henry VI or the new king, Edward IV?

Feeling that the tide had turned in his favour, Henry and his army crossed the border from Scotland into England, but they were defeated at the Battles of Hegeley Moor and Hexham.

Fleeing for his life Henry rode south and sought refuge for some time at Bolton Hall in Bowland, home of Sir Ralph Pudsay. This poor man, subject to fits of madness, could not remain from the authorities notice long, and soon circumstances forced him to leave Sir Ralph's home and flee to Waddington Hall, which at that time was the occasional residence of Sir John Tempest of Bracewell.

Sir John was married to a Talbot, and soon news of the arrival of the Lancastrian King came to the ears of Thomas Talbot of Bashall. The Talbots, eager to gain favour with King Edward, rode out in force and surrounded the Hall where the King was at dinner.

Upon hearing that the house was beset, Henry contrived to escape, and fled towards the river, hoping to put that between himself and his enemies. His pursuers, however, were too many and too eager for him. He was captured, after crossing the hipping stones, in a wood close by. From here he was conducted to London in the most ignominious manner, with his legs fastened to the stirrups of the sorry nag on which he was mounted, and an insulting placard fixed to his shoulders.

On July 9th, 1465, the Talbots were granted a reward for this service. Even today some see the Talbots' action as an act of treachery, but given those troubled times who is to say what was right or wrong?

Backridge

In Whitaker's 'History of Whalley' is a mention of an ancient battlefield at Backridge: "In a line betwixt Waddington and Bashall, but especially around Backridge, have been discovered many skeletons, which from the manner in which they lay, must indicate

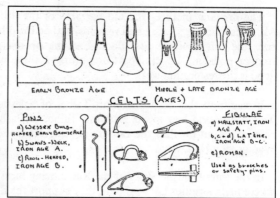

the place of some great engagement. Among the skeletons was found a broken celt, and some brass fibulae were discovered about the same time and place." In Whitaker's mind this was a battle between Romans and Celts.

Local tradition tells of the 'Battle of Bassas Brook', where King Arther and his forces defeated the Saxons under Tarquin forcing them back over the Pennines to York.

Others suppose it to be the site of the Battle of Brunanburh fought near a hill called Weondun, where there had been a pagan temple, in A.D. 937. At the hill fort of Brunanburh Athelstan defeated a Norse-British confederacy led by Anlaf of Dublin and Constantine, King of the Scots. The site has never been identified, and it may well be sited within Blackburnshire. Whatever the case Backridge holds its secrets well.

Bashall Hall to Edisford Hall

From the bridge walk up the drive to leave by the double field gate on the left. Walk up the hill to pass over stile to the left of the tall tree. Cross the Bashall Town to Backridge road and over the stile opposite. Walk down to pass over stile by gate. Cross the field on a slight right diagonal to go over ditch and on to go over footbridge and stile in hedge.

Walk up to the right, around hedgerow and on up and over to go over fence stile onto Cheetall farm lane. Pass over stile opposite and walk down to pass over corner fence stile. Follow left-hand fence to end of small wood. From here head for the right-hand corner of the field to pass over stile onto main road. Left, walk down to the junction. Edisford Hall is the farm on the right.

Edisford Hall

Edisford Hall stands upon the site of the Leper Hospital of Saint Nicholas. The hospital was founded by the burgesses of Clitheroe some time after 1140. The first charter of this hospital, undated, is one in which John, son of Ralph de Clitheroe granted three acres of land in Sidhill (Siddows) to the lepers in Edisford.

Another early charter, by Orme de Hammerton, granted "to God, St. Nicholas of the house of Edisford and to the brother lepers of the same dwelling with Reginald (warden) two acres on Schetill (Cheetall)". In 1211, Roger de Lacy, Constable of Chester, bequeathed to the hospital four acres of land in Baldwin Hill.

In c.1317, when Richard de Edisforth was warden, the house contained no lepers (the affliction of those poor men is now thought to have been elephantitis brought back from The Crusades in the East and not that of leprosy). Eventually, in 1351, the house having no staff or 'lepers', Hugh de Clitheroe, the bailiff, requested that the Abbot and Convent at Whalley take possession of the hospital and its lands.

The final notice of the hospital is in 1508 when John Paslew, the last abbot of Whalley, and the burgesses of Clitheroe jointly presented Sir William Heerd to the Chapel of St. Nicholas of Edisford, which was vacant as a result of the death of the previous holder of the office, Sir John Dineley.

Still to be made out in the stonework at the rear of the farmhouse are a number of shields set in Perpendicular arches bearing arms. In particular, note the lion rampant and fret of Roger de Lacy.

In the field across the way is the farm of Thirty Acres. It has a datestone of 1591 and a mullioned window, next to the porch, is also of that date.

Edisford Hall to Eadsford Bridge Car Park

Pass the Edisford Bridge Inn and walk down the road to cross Eadsford Bridge and follow footpath on right up to enter the car park.

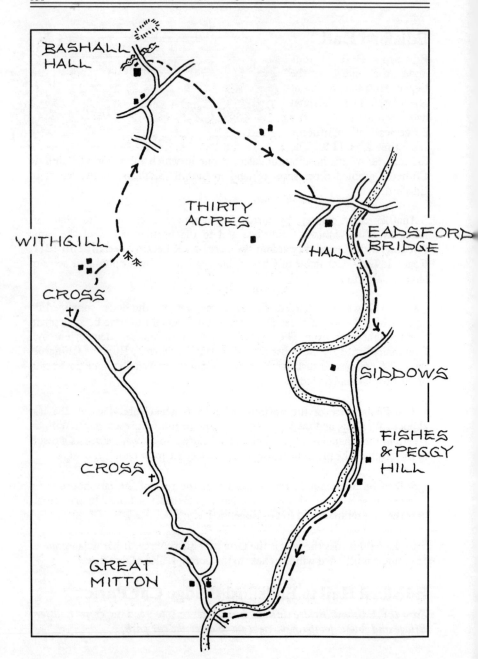

BASHALL
HALL

WITHGILL

THIRTY
ACRES

EADSFORD
BRIDGE

HALL

CROSS
†

SIDDOWS

CROSS †

FISHES
& PEGGY
HILL

GREAT
MITTON

8/11/93

Walk 14

OLD HALLS &
BATTLE GROUNDS

Siddows, Great Mitton, Withgill
and Bashall Hall

6 miles, 3 hours

MAP: *O.S. sheets SD 63/73 & 64/74 PATHFINDER*

LUNCH: *Three Fishes, Mitton, or*
The Edisford Bridge Hotel.

START: *Eadsford Bridge Car Park*

A circular walk from Eadsford Bridge down the Ribble to Mitton Magna to
return by way of Withgill and Bashall. Park your car on the car park on the
Clitheroe side of the bridge.

Eadsford Bridge to King's Mill/Siddows

Follow riverside pathway to go up over stile. Walk around the field to go over
stile onto Siddows Farm lane (a private road leads down to Siddows Farm).
Walk down the roadway, turn right and walk down to King's Mill).

Siddows

At Siddows once stood the King's Mill; sadly only a barn of this once great
enterprise stands today. The mill, owned by
the de Lacys, produced corn for seven
hundred years till c.1850.

The mill brought in a good revenue for the
de Lacys and when Clitheroe passed to the
Crown, King's Mill was leased out for a high
rent. Being the only mill on Crown property,

the miller had a monopoly. The mill's protective monopoly existed until the mid-19th century.

In the delightful garden of the house at Kings Mill can be found a keystone from the arched doorway of a barn that once stood here. It bears the date 1839 with the initials J.S.

Across the mill stream stands the ancient Siddows Farm with a full frontage of mullioned windows. A tablet above the door bears the date 1707 with the initials T:W:. At the time of writing this robust Jacobean farmhouse stands empty and forlorn, relegated to a mere junk store. Never has such a property cried out for preservation and restoration. The only survivor of the area's ancient past.

Kings Mill to Fishes and Peggy Hill

Walk on, past waste disposal centre and follow farm lane to Fishes and Peggy Hill (notice the stone tablet above the door displaying what could be fishes).

Fishes and Peggy Hill to Aspinall Arms

Walk on past Shuttleworth Farm, through gate to follow riverside pathway to aquaduct. Follow path on to go over footbridge at gap in line of trees. Walk up over a slight rise to go over a stile. Follow right-hand fence to go over a stile. Cross the field on right diagonal to go over stile and on to Aspinall Arms.

Aspinall Arms

The pub takes its name from the Aspinall family — landowners whose main house was Standen Hall.

Aspinall Arms to Great Mitton Hall

Follow the road over the bridge and up to Great Mitton Hall on the right.

Great Mitton

The tiny hamlet of Great Mitton is situated on a limestone rise above the River Ribble near to where it meets with the Hodder. Central to the settlement are the Church of All Hallows, The Old Hall and the Three Fishes Inn.

The Old Hall, with its rendered frontage, is easily overlooked by most visitors to the village and is best viewed from the rear or from the river bank at the Aspinall Arms.

Parts of the house go back to the 1350s, the outer porch doorway being a good example. The impressive gable-end belongs to the early 1600's with each floor sporting long mullioned windows. The curious gabled rear invites a closer inspection, but I suspect that this owes much to the 18th century.

The earliest record of a church at Mitton is in 1103 when Ralph the Red named himself as rector, after having been granted the manors of Bailey and Mitton the previous year. Of this early structure nothing remains. The present building was commenced in 1270 when the nave was built followed by the chancel in 1300. The tower and Shireburne Chapel date from 1438 and 1440 respectively, the latter was rebuilt in 1594 as it stands today by Richard Sherburne.

The church is Early English in style, about the end of this period. It is unusual in that one descends four steps into the church, the nave slopes downwards and there are more steps between the nave and the chancel. This is though not unique among the churches of England.

As was the custom at the time, Ralph as Lord of the Manor appointed himself Rector but had to have an ordained priest to take the services. This practice was abolished in 1215 and it led to the church being taken over by the Abbot of Cockersand Priory near Lancaster, who in 1241 appointed the incumbents.

In 1440 the Shireburne Chapel was built for masses and as a burial place for the Shireburnes, but there is no visible evidence that it was used for the latter purpose until 1594 when Sir Richard Shireburne was having the chapel rebuilt. He died the same year and is buried here along with his wife, Maud, in a beautiful alabaster tomb. The Shireburnes were descended from Ralph and lived at Stonyhurst House, now Stonyhurst College.

One Richard Shireburne built the almshouses on the fellside above Hurst Green which were moved to their present position in the village in 1947.

The tower dates from 1438 and now has six bells, the two earliest being inscribed with the year 1567. Alongside the walls of the nave are benches on which, before the pews were installed, the sick and disabled were allowed to sit, the present ones being replacements.

In its early days the church was the only one for some distance along the northern bank of the Ribble and therefore the Mother Church of the more recently built churches which now stand there, the oldest being Waddington which dates from 1438.

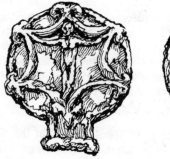 

MYTTON CHURCH

In the churchyard can be found, along with a stone coffin, a mounted cross-head of the 14th century depicting the Crucifixion of Christ set within some very finely carved tracery (though now in a poor state of preservation).

Over the doorway of the Three Fishes Inn are mounted a number of stones said to have come from Whalley Abbey. The perpendicular arches are correct, and the arms are those of Lacy.

THREE FISHES, MITTON

Three Fishes to Mitton Green Cross

Walk on past the Inn 200 paces to go over fence-stile on your right. Cross field directly, over fence-stile onto roadway, left and on, across junction to cross base.

Mitton Green Cross

Only a large pedestal remains of this former village cross. The cross stands at the foot of Toot Hill (place-name meaning 'look-out hill'). Many believe the area around Toot Hill to be the ancient site of the village of Mitton/Angerham given the large number of mediaeval coins and the like that have been found in the area by people with metal detectors (the use of which we deplore).

Mitton Green to Withgill Cross

Continue along the road, left at the junction, to the farm road on the right. The cross base is situated within the copse.

The Withgill Cross

Only the massive base pedestal of the old Withgill Cross remains today, and this is hidden from general view. In fact, for the last hundred years or so it was thought lost. It can be found in the coppice on the left of the entrance to Withgill Farm lane, ten feet inside the hedge bordering the Mitton to Bashall road, and is usually covered in undergrowth.

Up to around 1860, the pedestal stood by the roadway until a road-widening operation required its removal. The workmen at that time were told to break up the stone, but refused to do so given its religious associations, placing it out of the way behind the newly planted hedgerow.

The stone is covered in old graffiti and other marks, most prominent is a date of 1707 with the initials R.S. Another worked stone stands in the ditch 20m. up the farm lane. Could it be part of the cross shaft or could it be just a fragment of an old gate-post?

Withgill Cross to Bashall Hall

Walk up the farm lane, through the farmyard, up to the wood to enter the field on the left. Follow right-hand fence/hedgerow down, over stiles, to go through gate onto roadway. Walk up the lane opposite to Bashall town. Turn right and walk on to go left down the track to Bashall Hall Bridge.

Bashall Hall

The Talbots of Bashall were the parent stock of a once-great Lancashire family who held lands in Salesbury, Dinckley, Lower Darwen, Holt and Carrs, descended from one Geoffrey de Talbot, a Norman knight who was granted demesne land of the de Lacys at Bashall in 1250.

Over the bridge, in the field on the right, can be found the earthwork remains of the mediaeval fish ponds. A goit diverting the waters of Bassas Brook can also be made out. The establishing of fish ponds arose largely from the difficulty of getting fresh meat in the winter. Many villages, as well as monasteries and manors, had them and kept a variety of fish in them, including eels, as well as crayfish.

Bashall Hall stands on the banks of Bassas Brook where hereabouts an ancient battle is said to have taken place. Local tradition holds that the legendary Arthur defeated the incoming Saxons driving them back over the Pennines to Deria.

The finding of a number of skulls and other bones along with bronze weapons by the road at Backridge is said to be proof of the event. But, from a description of the bones and artefacts, it seems more likely that the road workers who discovered the finds had merely cut into a Bronze Age burial mound, there being many such sites in the immediate area.

Bashall Hall to Eadsford Bridge Car Park

Follow the directions given in "To Capture A King".

CLITHEROE CASTLE

The Place Name

Clitheroe is first mentioned in the Early Lancashire Charters of 1102, Clider-hou. The second element, 'hou', is Old Norse meaning hill 'haugr', the first, 'Clider', is Old English meaning a 'pile of stones or debris'. The place name suits the limestone crags on which the castle stands. A Megalithic structure may have once stood on the site given its prominence, but this is only surmise.

The ancient Lords of Salesbury and Bailey took Clitheroe as their family name — mediaeval decorated grave slabs of these can be found in Stydd Chapel and Sawley Abbey.

Clitheroe Castle: a description

The principal remnant of the castle is the small square Norman keep occupying a natural limestone knoll. There are early references to a castle here in 1102 and 1123-4, but these do not relate to any of the standing stone structures. Presumably the early castle was built of timber or, if of stone, did not include the keep.

The stone castle, including the keep, was probably the work of Roger de Lacy, Lord of the Honour of Pontefract in the years 1177-94. The keep is one of the smallest known, with the lower basement room only 17ft. square and the two floors above slightly larger (19 and 25ft. square), so that there was never a great deal of accommodation within. Entry is at first-floor level in the north-east wall, with a spiral staircase to the upper floor and the battlements in the north angle turret, and a small vaulted chamber in the west angle turret.

Alongside the latter is another entrance which communicated with the rampart walk of the surrounding curtain wall, the best portions being close to the keep which it encircles closely on three sides, like a chemise (a wall surrounding the base of the keep).

Towards the south the curtain swung away to enclose a triangular bailey, the area of which is now mostly occupied by later buildings of Georgian and later mediaeval dress. Lord Torrington in 1792 wrote of 'a foolishly fancied Gothic house'. How much of genuine mediaeval survives around the houses and the walls has not been sorted out yet.

CLITHEROE CASTLE
C. 1723

Clitheroe Castle: a history

Around 1072, after the 1069 rebellion in the North, Duke William of Normandy added Amounderness and the lands between the Mersey and Ribble to lands already possessed by Roger de Poitou.

These lands along with Furness, Lonsdale and Cartmel made up a 'buffer zone' against the Scottish invaders. Roger, as Lord of Lancaster, built castles and created a number of military fiefs giving unity to an area later to be known as Lancashire. It is thought that in the early 12th century he had a motte and bailey fortification of timber erected on the summit of the limestone outcrop at Clitheroe.

In 1102, Robert de Belleme, supported by his brother Roger de Poitou, led an unsuccessful rebellion against Henry I. This led to the confiscation of Roger's English estates.

The Honor of Lancaster was then granted to Stephen of Blois. The castle and the honor of Clitheroe was then granted to Ilbert de Lacy and remained in the estates of the de Lacy family until the death of Henry de Lacy, Earl of Lincoln, in 1310.

The castle got its first taste of warfare in 1138 when King David of Scotland led his army on a raid into England. He detached part of his army into Yorkshire under his nephew William fitz Duncan. With great carnage the Scots laid waste the monastery of Furness and the province of Craven with fire and sword.

On the 10th June that year William was attacked by the forces of King Stephen at Eadsford Bridge near Clitheroe. The English force was routed with the spilling of much blood, the castle was taken but its contents amounted to little.

In 1315, Adam Banastre forefronted a rebellion of Northern lords. During this period he seized the castle at Clitheroe and the weapons held there, a few bows and pikes, no great spoil as at this time the castle's main use was as a prison, being governed by a constable.

For a brief period during the Civil Wars Prince Rupert held the fortification for the Royalist cause. In 1644 Rupert passed through Clitheroe on his way to Skipton Castle.

He left Colonel Daniel as governor of the castle who in turn placed Captain Cuthbert Bradkirk of Wrea in charge. Bradkirk repaired the Gate House and outer walls and stocked the keep with provisions.

After the battle of Marston Moor the castle was abandoned by the Royalists and for a short time it was occupied by a Parliamentarian force. In 1649 it was for the most part destroyed and the keep reduced to a ruin upon the orders of Major General Lambert.

The castle chapel, that appears to have been maintained until the Civil War, also fell into ruin, the chaplains allowance thenceforward annexed to the curacy of the Parish Church of St. Mary Magdalene.

Castle Parish

Inside the inner bailey of Clitheroe Castle stood the Chapel of St. Michael the Archangel coeval with the foundation of the castle, erected and amply endowed by the founder, with licence of the Dean of Whalley, for the purpose of having Divine service performed, and the sacraments administered to the household, servants and foresters.

This is proved by the charter of Guy de la Val, the immediate grantee after the attainder of Robert de Lacy, which conveys to the priory of St. John of Kirkby (Pontefract), amongst other things, the 'chapel of my castle of Clitheroe' c. 1120.

The chapel was sometimes called extra-parochial and sometimes described as the parish church of the castle and demesne, with the large forest districts of the honor. In either case it was outside the parish of Whalley ecclesiastically, but the convent, after long contention, had it awarded to them in 1349, but it was not till 1365 that the monks finally obtained possession from John of Gaunt.

They treated the forest district of which it was the head as a peculiar jurisdiction, holding regular visitations for it in place of the bishop.

These courts were held sometimes in Whalley Church and sometimes in the castle chapel itself; the principal matters dealt with were marriage cases, proofs of wills, immorality, working on Holy Days, and minor offences, such as talking in church.

What follows is a list of the known incumbents of Castle Parish:

William de Nunny 1311

William Chaillon 1321

Richard Camel 1322

Roger de Lysewy 1322

Richard de Moseley 1334

Henry de Walton 1349

John de Stafford 1365

The places under the jurisdiction of Castle Parish were the forest areas being Pendle, Rossendale, Trawden, Bowland, Chatburn, Clitheroe Castle, Ramsgreave end Hoddlesden. The tithes from these forest areas would be

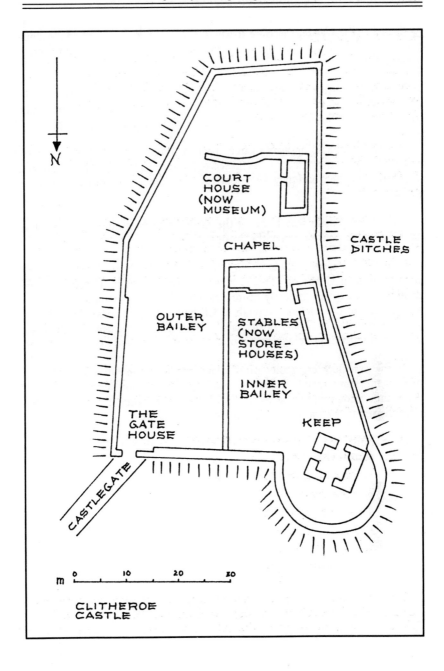

N

COURT
HOUSE
(NOW
MUSEUM)

CASTLE
DITCHES

CHAPEL

OUTER
BAILEY

STABLES
(NOW
STORE-
HOUSES)

INNER
BAILEY

THE
GATE
HOUSE

KEEP

CASTLEGATE

m 0   10   20   30

CLITHEROE
CASTLE

collected at the Castle, therefore it would not, I think, be too presumptuous to see the Castle Keep as a giant stone money-box for holding the Forest revenues.

After the Reformation its dependent chapels of Newchurch-in-Pendle, New-church-in-Rossendale and Whitewell-in-Bowland became parochial, the latter receiving the dedication and revenue formerly given to the mother chapel.

The Castle chapel appears to have been maintained until the Civil War, when from after that time it was allowed to fall into ruin. In 1717 nothing but the walls remained, and they were decayed. The chapel is not mentioned in the visitation lists.

Since 1895, Castle Parish, being the castle and surrounding grounds, has been under the jurisdiction of the Borough Authorities.

Within the Castle walls is Castle House, once the home of the Steward of the honor of Clitheroe. This is now the town Museum. Displays on the ground floor explain the early history of the valley and surrounding areas as well as that of the ancient Borough of Clitheroe. Local trades and crafts are also illustrated in a variety of displays of tools and equipment and there are also reconstructions of cloggers and printers workshops, and a cottage interior.

On the first floor are geological displays recording the story of Salthill, an ancient limestone reef now quarried out. It is vividly portrayed by means of panoramic photographs and examples of the many forms of marine life that once thrived in the warm seas that once covered this area.

The Salthill Quarry Trail is one of the few geological trails in the country and well worth a visit.

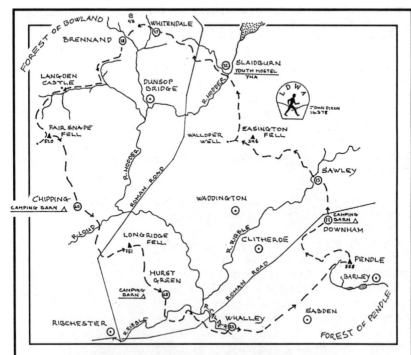

THE BOWLAND-PENDLE CHALLENGE TRAIL
85km — 53 miles

This Long Distance Trail that circumnavigates an Area of Outstanding Natural Beauty has been devised by John Dixon as a 24-hour challenge walk. It can be linked with the 47-mile Pendle Way to make a 'figure of eight' 100-mile two-day challenge. Alternatively, the Trail can be done over two or four days using YHA Camping Barns.

The Trail passes below the Whitendale Hanging Stones, above Dunsop Bridge, the official Ordnance Survey Centre of Britain.

For an illustrated guide, giving walking directions, gradient profile, details on Camping Barns and the Bowland-Pendle Challenge Certificate/Badge, send £3.75 to John Dixon, 8 Back Skipton Road, Barnoldswick, Lancashire BB8 5NE.